EDITED BY STEPHEN JENKINS

FRITZ LANG
The Image and the Look

1981
BFI Publishing

Cover design: Sue Molineux (Gloria Grahame and Glenn Ford in *The Big Heat*)

Published by the British Film Institute A11510
127 Charing Cross Road
London WC2H OEA

ISBN 0 85170 108 6 (hardcover)
    0 85170 109 4 (paperback)

Printed in England by Tonbridge Printers Ltd, Tonbridge, Kent

Contents

Acknowledgments

I would like to thank the following individuals and organisations for their assistance: Lindsey Boyd, David Wilson, David Meeker, Tom Milne, Erich Sargeant, Paul Willemen, Martin Wright, BFI Film and Video Library (Nigel Algar), Contemporary Films (Lotte Steinhart), Harris/Films (Syd Saville, Philip Strick), National Film Archive (Elaine Burrows). Thanks also to Enno Patalas and Peter Syr of the Munich Film Museum for supplying eight of the frame blow-ups (which originally appeared in the Reihe Hanser book *Fritz Lang*). Acknowledgment is made to the respective production and distribution companies of the films illustrated in this book.

STEPHEN JENKINS

Introduction

The Lang-text, that group of films which bears the name of Fritz Lang as director, has long served to expose the problems and contradictions inherent in conventional notions of authorship. By the latter I mean the desire to bind together a collection of individual film texts under an authorial heading, the imaginary unity signified by the name following the 'directed by' credit.

For the British critical/journalistic establishment this desire was thwarted in the case of Lang by the biographical fact of his flight in 1933 from Germany and the Nazis to America and Hollywood. The German production context of the 1920s and early 1930s was associated with 'art' (a mixture of epic Romanticism and Expressionism), and a handful of individual texts, such as *Die Nibelungen, Metropolis* and *M*, were granted the status of 'classics' in various versions of the history of the cinema. The problem posed for critics was how to deal with Lang as author/artist within the context of the Hollywood process. The answer, predictably, was to see him as artistically in decline, and to regard this section of his work as showing only brief flashes of 'genius'. The fissure could be bridged in part by pointing to the overt social seriousness of the content of his first two American films (the problem of mob violence in *Fury*, the problem of society's attitude to ex-convicts in *You Only Live Once*), while at the same time indicating that the relationship of these films to the socially conscious American cinema of the 30s was problematic. In this way the separation of the artist from the production context/process was maintained.

But such a separation could only be maintained negatively as regards the director's films of the 40s and 50s, his most productive American period, in that Lang's artistic presence was acknowledged, but only as a memory, as something visually absent, a lack. The desire to confuse the person Fritz Lang with what was signified by the name 'Fritz Lang' as it occurred across a number of texts led, as usual, to the fetishisation of the person at the expense of serious consideration of the texts themselves and to the usual irrelevant dead-end questioning. 'One doesn't know whether in the last eight years, Lang has found difficulty in obtaining congenial subjects, or whether the conventionality of much of his output has reflected an inner lassitude,' wrote Gavin Lambert ('Fritz Lang's America', *Sight and Sound*, Summer/Autumn 1955). In fact the director,

1

and the films, were simply victims of the critical establishment's refusal to deal seriously with the bulk of the product of the American cinema. Superficial readings of ostensible narrative content enabled these critics to consign Lang's work to the realms of 'workmanlike commerce' or 'sterile artiness' (Lambert again). Needless to say, this attitude is still prevalent. In his obituary of Lang in the *Financial Times* (6 August 1976), Nigel Andrews, having constructed his fantasy of the person Lang ('in many ways everyone's favourite idea of a film director. The jodphurs, the riding boots, the clipped Teutonic manner'), described most of his American work as 'superior hack pieces', and fell back on the cliché that 'the most fruitful phase of Lang's career was undoubtedly his German period'.

However, the Lang text has also been an important focus of attention for other writings, which we might link in that they subscribe to that version of authorship known historically as *la politique des auteurs*. For French critics of the 50s, including Godard, Truffaut, Rohmer, Rivette and Chabrol, Lang's oeuvre became a perfect cause to champion in their campaign to assert the merits of the American popular cinema. Not only could they trace the constancy of certain themes running through the films directed by Lang on both sides of the Atlantic, but they could also polemically proclaim the American films as being superior, especially in terms of their *mise en scène*. As Jean Domarchi wrote of *While the City Sleeps*: 'I protest against the disrepute which affects the American output of this author . . . In fact Lang has found, with a perfected American technique, the consummate expression of his talent. He is less of a great painter than Murnau, and American methods have allowed him to rid himself of Expressionist bric-à-brac, to arrive at an unsurpassable rigour . . . free of all excrescences and all the naivety which burdened *Siegfrieds Tod* or *Metropolis.' (Cahiers du Cinéma*, October 1956).

For the French writers this rigour took the form of a gradually more austere and precise sense of *mise en scène*. What British critics read as Lang's lack of interest in the shoddy material foisted upon him in the Hollywood factory, the French saw as a metaphysical detachment, a lack of interest in any notions of psychological or material naturalism, entirely fitting for the depiction of a world governed by a sense of fatalism. Great importance was placed on the fact of Lang's early training as an architect: 'His thematic, the fatality of the fall, vengeance, the occult power of secret societies and the networks of espionage, has no more importance in his eyes than his aesthetic, which illustrates and produces it, surrounding the characters with a frame of which they are the slaves . . . The decor, even the edges of the screen, have, in their design, as much importance as the actors . . . The work of Fritz Lang is based on a metaphysic of architecture.' (Claude Chabrol, *Cahiers du Cinéma*, December 1955).

A film like *Beyond a Reasonable Doubt* could thus be read by Jacques

Rivette as a culmination of this sense of detachment, whereby what is striking is 'the diagrammatic, or rather expository aspect instantly assumed by the unfolding of the images: as though what we were watching were less the *mise en scène* of a script than simply the reading of the script, presented to us just as it is, without embellishment. Without personal comment of any kind on the part of the storyteller either. So one might be tempted to talk about a purely objective *mise en scène*, if such a thing were possible'. (*Cahiers du Cinéma*, November 1957, translated in the BFI publication *Jacques Rivette: Text and Interviews*). Which leads to the contradiction of the perfect *mise en scène* being no *mise en scène* at all, the impossible interface of precise, cold, analytic detachment and the objectivity constantly denied by the basic fact of the cinema as signifying process.

While the French critics differed in their opinions as regards the merits of certain Lang films, particularly *The Tiger of Eschnapur* and *The Indian Tomb*, their general attitude had an inevitable knock-on effect on later British and American writings on the director's work. Writers like Andrew Sarris in *The America Cinema* (1968), Peter Bogdanovich in *Fritz Lang in America* (1967), and Colin McArthur in *Underworld USA* (1972) all reacted consciously against the position adopted by earlier critics. The problem was that none of them really went beyond the French version of auteurism. Bogdanovich criticised 'Lambert and other Grierson-minded critics' precisely because for them 'a film is not examined for how much of the artist is exposed, but for how much of society'. But the auteurist game of piecing together the supposed world view of 'the artist' on the basis of meanings extracted from individual texts is hardly revealed as a more constructive attitude on the basis of what was discerned in Lang's work. Lang's remark to Bogdanovich concerning 'the main characteristic, the main theme that runs through all my pictures — this fight against destiny, against fate' was seized upon by these writers as the key to the man and the films, two entities which were then telescoped together. Thus for Sarris, 'Lang is determinism', and his films are 'the product of a bleak view of the universe where man grapples with his personal destiny and loses'. For Bogdanovich, 'Lang's work has been remarkably consistent over the years, both in theme and outlook: the fight against fate continues from *Der müde Tod* . . . to *Beyond a Reasonable Doubt*'. And McArthur writes of 'the despair of mankind, the sense of evil and of omnipotent forces at work, which forms the necessary starting point for an understanding of Lang's films'. But this abstracted idea of fate as a governing principle, when allied to an unquestioning auteurist stance, means that the films are read basically as self-satisfying expressions of a certain Germanic frame of mind, an *angst*, which Lang himself described as the making of a 'fetish of tragedy'. As a result, they are seen to signify nothing but that *angst*. According to McArthur, 'It is difficult to resist the conviction that the physical presence of urban

3

America and the country's *mores* confirmed Lang's despair'. Bogdanovich claims that 'The tears he [Lang] elicits for the damned figures who inhabit it [his world]... are born from the depths of his personality'. And Sarris concludes that 'in a century that has spawned Hitler and Hiroshima, no artist can be called paranoiac, he *is* being persecuted'.

While writings of this kind had a polemic value, in that they paid some serious attention to the latter half of the Lang-text, ultimately they came to a dead-end as regards anything other than descriptions of the person Lang's world-view, as manifested thematically and stylistically through a body of work. The text becomes only a coherent, well-ordered signifier of despair. In order to move beyond this idea it is perhaps the very notion of coherence itself which needs to be deconstructed and historically located. Raymond Bellour, in his essay *On Fritz Lang*, writes: 'Lang plays a highly perverse game. It is through the lacunae, the lack he establishes, that he seems intelligible.' Yet it is noticeable that those writers previously cited who have attempted to deal positively with the Lang-text have done so by sealing over, for example, what might be read as the primary fissure within that text, i.e. the gap between the German and American work.

This sealing over is generally accomplished by treating the text either as a thematically coherent whole (the notion that the world view remains constant whatever the production context), or as an evolving entity (the 'trappings' of Expressionism become something gradually cast off by Lang as his art progresses). Both these views assume that the crucial factor in 'understanding' the text is to detect the presence of the authorial subject from whom it stems, and by virtue of whom it coheres. Both text and authorial subject lie somewhere 'out there', waiting, unchanging, to be deciphered. Yet, clearly, these auteurist readings of (the) Lang (text) themselves exist only within a historical chain of criticism, each link of which produces a different version of that text, which has no existence outside the reading which produces it. In this sense the closing of the fissure can be seen as historically determined by the particular cultural context which produced the auteurist approach to the American cinema. In the same way the British critics of the 40s and 50s *stressed* the gap, 'Lang' as a memory held over from the German films, an attitude produced as a result of the context within which *they* were writing.

In fact, if one considers what the British critics (exemplified here by quotes from reviews in the British Film Institute's *Monthly Film Bulletin*) found wrong with Lang's American and last German films, then one discovers that the version of that half of the text which they construct is not very different from later auteurist versions; the terms are similar, simply expressed negatively. For example, Lang's rigorous anti-naturalism, and seeming indifference to verisimilitude, is seized upon repeatedly:

4

'an efficient production department . . . falls down badly in trying to present air raid scenes . . . the presentation of them is rather ludicrous if not distasteful' (*Ministry of Fear*)
'unconvincing and melodramatic film' (*Secret Beyond the Door*)
'a succession of theatrically handled episodes' (*House by the River*)
'Although the Technicolor jungle may be taken as authentic very little else rings true . . . the highly artificial love affair between players who never escape from stock situations' (*American Guerilla in the Philippines*)
'The film in fact relies on a series of tricks and coincidences beginning with its entirely implausible central situation . . . This is thriller construction on a one dimensional level' (*Beyond a Reasonable Doubt*).

Hand in hand with this goes the unconcern for 'depth of character', at the level of either script or performance:

'The low key camera work insists on flapping curtains for the foreground interest of practically every shot. Lang seems to be more concerned with these than characters' (*House by the River*)
'It promises more than it provides in the way of characterisation' (*Rancho Notorious*)
'Lang might have been expected . . . to extract more enterprising performances from such experienced players' (*Blue Gardenia*)
'automatic performances' (*Human Desire*)
'the dramatics are weakened by shallow characterisation' (*While the City Sleeps*)
'the playing also tends to be fairly mechanical' (*Beyond a Reasonable Doubt*)
'the inadequacies of his cast' (*1000 Eyes of Dr Mabuse*).

Bellour suggests that a certain formal play at the level of individual shots means that 'at the film's other extreme, as it were, Lang this time plays the counter-game against the script. Since he throws his images off-balance by extending them, he throws his narrative off course.' British critics seemed to detect something similar but, again, expressed it in negative terms, as a 'failure' in the handling of narrative, as regards economy, excitement, tension, etc.:

'It tends to be overlong' (*Hangmen Also Die*)
'It seems that when the talents of directors are in decline their pictures become exceptionally slow' (*House by the River*)
'the picture lacks the excitement which Fritz Lang's name on the credits would once have assured' (*American Guerilla in the Philippines*)
'far from exciting thriller . . . Lang might have been expected to bring a good deal more dramatic tension to the situation' (*The Blue Gardenia*)
'Fritz Lang seems to have lost most of his old power to sustain

5

dramatic tension' (*The Big Heat*)
'deficient in dramatic tension' (*Moonfleet*)
'a certain heaviness in the actual narrative style' (*1000 Eyes of Dr Mabuse*).

Auteurists seized on factors like these as the mark of the Langian presence on the individual film texts, and used them to develop their idea of Lang's 'world view'. The British critics were caught in a curious dilemma. Lang was associated with 'art', Hollywood with product. The gap could occasionally be bridged, when the subject of a Hollywood film was overtly 'serious', or alternatively Hollywood could produce superior, polished, well-formed entertainment. But Lang's work failed on both counts. It was locked into various traditional Hollywood genres (thrillers, war films, westerns, etc.), and therefore not 'serious'; but at the same time it did not offer particularly achieved examples of these genres. It seemed to fail both as art and as entertainment, and as a result the idea of Lang as a controlling, identifiable directorial presence tended to disappear from the critical discourse:

'though direction is clever it is not as outstanding as one would expect' (*Woman in the Window*)
'direction is not quite as remarkable as one would expect' (*Cloak and Dagger*)
'bears little sign of Fritz Lang's former greatness' (*Secret Beyond the Door*)
'It is difficult to accept the evidence of the credits that this . . . was directed by Fritz Lang' (*The Blue Gardenia*)
'the film as a whole is far from being one of the director's more personal works. The handling is cold blooded and conventionally contrived' (*Beyond a Reasonable Doubt*).

On the basis of similar findings, one reading creates Lang, the other causes him to disappear.

While it is clear that auteurism can be seen as a more productive basis for engagement with the latter half of the Lang-text, as opposed to the earlier British stance which precisely refused to engage with it, which dismissed it as unworthy of serious critical attention, nevertheless the obvious must be stressed: auteurism cannot account definitively for the Lang-text since this goal is impossible. The text is created anew with every reading of it. The problem is not 'Lang' but auteurism itself. Auteurism is not simply a critical movement, one of a series, that can be located historically, and that has been succeeded by an interest in semiotics, structuralism, psycho-analysis, etc.; rather it is a concept which shifts and changes but in which film culture's investment at all levels remains constant. Retrospectives of directors' work, books on directors, still proliferate, some marked by an awareness of developments in film theory, some not, but all marked by the names of Ophuls, Dreyer, Aldrich, Lang, etc.

What must be made explicit is what does the name signify? What is signified here by the name Lang? While it is obviously not biography, not the person Lang, neither is it, to use Peter Wollen's distinction from *Signs and Meaning in the Cinema*, 'Lang' the structure named after him, since this implies that such a structure exists, as something to be grasped. 'Lang' here is a space where a multiplicity of discourses intersect, an unstable, shifting configuration of discourses produced by the interaction of a specific group of films (Lang's filmography) with particular, historically and socially locatable ways of reading/ viewing those films. I hope this collection of writings will begin to trace some sort of useful path through that space.

Lang and Auteurism

The articles by Michel Mourlet and Philippe Demonsablon which follow these notes originally appeared in *Cahiers du Cinéma* no.99 (September 1959), and have been included as examples of *la politique des auteurs* in full cry. This particular issue of the magazine also included an interview with Lang, by Rivette and Jean Domarchi, a long review of *The Indian Tomb*, and a Lang bio-filmography. This Lang-centred auteurist thrust dictated the nature of the rest of the magazine's contents — an article on Hitchcock by Jean Douchet, reviews of McCarey's *Rally Round the Flag Boys*, Minnelli's *The Reluctant Debutante*, and Cottafavi's *Revolt of the Gladiators*. Even Luc Moullet's report on the San Sebastian Film Festival claimed that the event's existence was justified by the screening of *North by Northwest*.

The critical neglect which the Lang-text suffered in Britain was in a sense inevitable, and had little to do with Lang in particular. It had to do with dominant attitudes towards the American cinema in general, towards auteurism and *mise en scène* criticism, and indeed towards *Cahiers*. One might usefully note here the contents of *Sight and Sound's* double issue for Summer/Autumn 1959, which provides a striking contrast to the French publication. Included were articles on the 'explosion' of New Wave films at the Cannes festival, on the influx of television 'talent' into the American cinema, on comedy, on *Look Back in Anger*, a letter from Jonas Mekas on American independent productions, a translation of a poem by Brecht, an interview with Visconti, a piece by Kozintsev, etc. The review pages are dominated by *We Are the Lambeth Boys*, *Les Cousins*, *Ashes and Diamonds*, *The Face* and *Le Amiche*. The fact that *Anatomy of a Murder* is covered means little — so are Delbert Mann's *Middle of the Night* and Zinnemann's *The Nun's Story*. Perhaps the most significant review, however, is Penelope Houston on *North by Northwest*, which includes the following: 'Critics who like to see Hitchcock's films as so many cryptograms to be puzzled over for hidden symbols are going to have a hard time with *North by Northwest*. This is the greatest piece of entertainment film-making we have had from him in years.'

The response to what can be read as an almost overt challenge to *Cahiers* appeared in issue 102, where Luc Moullet's long article on the film centres not on its entertainment value, but on the question of Hitchcock and Catholicism. In the same issue Wajda's *Ashes and*

Diamonds is coolly dismissed as the work of a director with 'a taste for exhibitionism'. Fellini, Kazan, Vadim and Bergman also suffer from the desire to deal with 'subjects which will give free rein to their inveterate narcissism'. Wajda's work does not evince 'the flashes of cinematic brilliance which allow a Franju or a Nicholas Ray to overcome their neuroses'. If one flashes back to the previously mentioned *Sight and Sound* review of the same film, one finds the narcissistic neurotic transformed, predictably, into the lonely, suffering artist: 'His faith no longer strikes one as a search undertaken in hope, but as a lonely, losing struggle against misanthropy and disillusion. One thing above all seems to keep him going: a burning desire to express all that is young, mortal, sentient and suffering in an absolute orgy of self-identification.'

The basic oppositions which emerge from all this (art cinema/popular culture, Europe/Hollywood, pluralism/auteurism) are to a degree deceptive. The issue of *Sight and Sound* did include an auteur-oriented article on the American cinema and an interview with Robert Siodmak. The next issue of *Cahiers* (no. 100) carried articles by Bergman, Renoir and Cocteau. Nevertheless, Mourlet and Demonsablon's pieces are representative of the kind of French writing which *Sight and Sound* considered alien enough to warrant explanation/attack on behalf of its readers. And inevitably the magazine's own *politique* (usually disguised as 'common sense'), of which the Lang-text was one of many victims, was implicitly articulated. In his article 'The French Line' (*Sight and Sound*, Autumn 1960) Richard Roud notes that films such as *Vertigo, Run of the Arrow, A Time to Love and a Time to Die,* and *Wind Across the Everglades* had appeared in various *Cahiers* critics' '10 Best' lists for the year. He states that 'One's first reaction might be to conclude that these men must be very foolish'. Similarly, the fact that Lang's *Moonfleet* was awarded the prize for best foreign film of the year in the 'Prix de la Nouvelle Critique' (beating *Pather Panchali* into second place) is expected to provoke a *Sight and Sound* reader into 'throwing up one's hands in the air, or dismissing them [the French critics] as mad'. What makes such responses problematic is that 'by and large the tastes of the *Cahiers* team of critics coincide with ours [and] that some of them have made remarkable and even great films'. The 'problem' is solved as Roud explains how and why 'American life in all its forms exercises a very strong hold over the present-day young French intellectuals'. And while 'among the older of the *Cahiers* critics, the films they make themselves correspond more to what we in England like to think of as great cinema: a fusion of significant form with literary or humanistic content . . . among some of the newer (as yet, non-film-making) members of the *Cahiers* team, Hollywood is regarded as *the* cinema'. This is seen as obviously misguided, doubly so because inflected by the fanatical application of the *politique des auteurs* (described by Roud as 'idolatry'), and an obsession with *mise en scène* ('the greatest difference between *Cahiers du Cinéma* and this magazine: if driven

9

to it, *Cahiers* will choose form and *Sight and Sound* content'). The Mourlet article provides the perfect example of what Roud was attacking/ explaining: 'Lang's climactic period began in 1948 with a *mise en scène* which ceased being a prop for the script or a superficial decoration of space to become intense and inward, calling settings and people into question, predicated upon such fundamental problems as eyes, hand movements, the subtle illumination of abysses. Here the script supports the *mise en scène*, which becomes the end.'

Roud's position becomes clear when he states: 'There is nothing wrong with this purist theory. A critic should try to separate the literary qualities of a scenario or the intellectual qualities of a story from the purely formal qualities of a film — the way in which "the actors and the objects, and their movement within the frame" express the personality, the genius of a director. The trouble, it seems to me, is in their application of this theory. For to these critics, the great film of 1960 . . . was Nicholas Ray's *Party Girl.*' In other words, whatever one thinks of the theory in question, common sense tells us where it should, or, more important, should not be applied. This basically comes down to the distinction between non-Hollywood and Hollywood films, where intellectualising and theory either is or is not appropriate. Again Roud becomes explicit on this point: 'Unfortunately, when a critic has to quote Hegel and Kant in reviewing a film by Minnelli, it is not because, as Hoveyda [a *Cahiers* critic] maintains, the cinema is at least as important as literature, painting and the drama. It is because somehow the critic feels he must dignify his liking of the film by the most impeccable intellectual references . . . The trouble, one feels, is that they [the French critics] like the second-rate but daren't admit it, so the second-rate must be built up by dint of references to Kant, Hegel *et al.*' According to this logic the references to Euclid, Hegel, Pascal, Mallarmé, Heraclitus, Valéry and Goethe which occur within the two Lang articles are signs of the 'second-rateness' of the Lang text, a quality mystically discerned through the critical theory known as common sense.

In fact, the articles clearly demonstrate what Roud himself described elsewhere (*Sight and Sound*, Summer/Autumn 1959) as being 'essential for a proper understanding of French film criticism [i.e., to realise] the enormous prestige attached to philosophical interpretation, aesthetic theorising and formal analysis', all couched here in terms of an obsession with the author/director/subject as the absolute source of meaning. It is of course the idea of author as unproblematic subject, the 'point' of these articles, which would be radically displaced by later developments in film theory, around the areas of semiotics, structuralism, psychoanalysis, etc. But the celebration of an authorial system at least permits the consideration of the Lang-text as a whole, made up of elements which relate inwardly toward each other, 'a circle imprisoning a universe that is sufficient unto itself' to quote Mourlet, a specifically filmic discourse. Hence the references cited above to *other discourses* (rather than an appeal to an unproblematic, commonsense experience of reality — see below) through which the pleasure of the text is articulated.

It was this double referential movement (inward into the authorial system, outward to other systems, filmic and otherwise) which *Sight and Sound* found unacceptable. In 'The Critical Question' (also from the Autumn 1960 issue) Penelope Houston laid the differences on the line. This was largely in response to writings appearing at the time in the magazine *Oxford Opinion*, *Cahiers*-influenced and in turn, crucially for British film culture, leading to *Movie*. According to this article: 'the weakness of the *Cahiers* school, both in its own country, and among its exponents here, seems to be that it barely admits of experience which does not take place in the cinema . . . it turns inward upon itself, so that a film's validity is assessed not in relation to the society from which it draws its material but in relation to other cinematic experiences. It is all a bit hermetic . . .' It is the posited alternative to the 'hermetic' approach which explains the resounding silence around the Lang and other texts: 'You cannot write, for instance, about a film like *Pather Panchali* (or *Les 400 Coups*, or *Tokyo Story*) without concerning yourself with the way in which certain truths about the relationships between people, and the place of these people in their society, are defined on the screen.' The idea that 'The film is not enclosed within its circumference . . . Cinema is about human relationships, not about "spatial relationships" could be a direct reply to Mourlet. But such an idea constitutes an effective refusal to speak about the Lang-text, which is composed precisely of 'films whose relation to the business of living is in itself somewhat precarious' (to say the very least). Nevertheless, in its attempt to articulate the concerns of what it calls the 'new critical school' the article does provide a concise introduction to the following pieces: 'There are no good or bad subjects; affirmation is a word for boy scouts; social significance is a bore; don't expect a film to present you with sympathetic characters; don't even, if one takes it far enough, look for character; don't have any truck with anything that smacks of literature . . .' s.j.

MICHEL MOURLET

Fritz Lang's Trajectory

(originally published in Cahiers du Cinéma, *no. 99, September 1959)*

What is a film but an implacable and inevitable flow of images into which the fascinated consciousness plunges, forgetting self and discovering the heart of existence? Fritz Lang is one of the few to have fully fathomed and resolved this question, what is a film, raised by the work of the great film-makers. His entire *oeuvre* looms as a slow and stubborn progress, once the ends have been posed, towards perfecting the means capable of leading to these ends. What are these ends? As in any work of art, to impose a certain condition of the world with maximum intensity, in such a way that patent revelation will inhibit critical reflexes. The cinema being a view of things, and especially of people, there is good reason for imposing upon appearances a movement such that, caught in the machinery, the spectator's consciousness will become the passive locus of a liturgy in which each gesture reflects the totality of the symbol. The film will then be entirely closed in upon itself, a circle imprisoning a universe that is sufficient unto itself, because any possible withdrawal would arise within an interference fringe between the film and everyday reality (whether occasioned by a rejection of the banal as pointless, the chancy as damaging, or the false as ineffectual). If the banal and the false awaken the spectator from his hypnotic sleep and restore him to his present reality, what field is left to cultivate? The only answer is: what is possible, in other words what is perceived to be both true and extraordinary, as a realisation of potentialities, quenching man's primordial thirst. And if contingency disrupts the unity of the work and disperses its power, an organisation of what is possible as *inevitable,* in such a way that the film ineluctably assaults the spectator's expectations, leads us to the heart of Lang's problem. The elimination of chance, the constant domination of forms by an architecture in which each part determines and is answerable to the others, result in a fascination or an inability in the spectator to escape the discipline of the film.

*   *   *

Not surprisingly, Fritz Lang's *oeuvre* has followed a path which is none other than the one taken by the cinema itself, seen as a whole. The means he has placed at the service of his ends reveal both their permanence and a sense of transformation. From *Die Spinnen* to *Frau im Mond* an aesthetic is outlined which naturally took its basic elements from the state of the contemporary cinema: its silence, in particular, felt as a lack and compensated for by distorting appearances into visual metaphors. What was to become a geometry of souls had to limit itself at first to a geometry of space. Expressionism was cast into a Euclidean mould which transformed its meaning. Unable as yet to encompass beings and expose their very depths, Lang extrapolated their movements towards a decorative blueprint whose ordinances were symmetry and slowness. So a liturgy was created, based on a purely formal hieratism. Already the principal feature of Lang's later attitude to actors is prefigured in this liturgy, where they are its servants: in other words, turning them into a completely neutralised vehicle for *mise en scène* considered as pure movement, whereas the reverse is generally true of other film-makers, for whom *mise en scène* is a means to glorify the actors rather as the flow of an imponderable current lights up electric bulbs. Hence Lang's predilection for actors who are more negative than positive, and whose reticence, diffidence or passivity more readily suffers the annihilation imposed on them (Dana Andrews, Glenn Ford, Walter Reyer . . .).

The cinema's access to the world of sound seemed to disorient Lang, who lost sight of the rigour he had sought and instead devoted himself to ideas, to demonstration, to the impurity of moral postulates intervening in the relationships between people and falsifying them. *M* and *You Only Live Once*, among others, reflect this relaxation caused by an intoxication with speech as yet neither mastered nor integrated with a more inner-directed *mise en scène* developing the geometrical premises of the silent period. One has to wait until after the war to find this achievement outlined in *Ministry of Fear* and *Rancho Notorious*, flowering in *Secret Beyond the Door*, *The Big Heat*, *Human Desire*, *While the City Sleeps*, *Moonfleet* and *Beyond a Reasonable Doubt*, and culminating in the complete maturity and summation of *The Tiger of Eschnapur* and *The Indian Tomb*. It goes without saying that the trajectory thus described is not quite so straightforward in detail if looked at more closely. There are breaks, leaps forward followed by relapses. Thus the two parts of *Dr Mabuse the Gambler* have a more modern tone than *Die Nibelungen* or *Metropolis*. *Fury*, although Lang's first film in America, is nevertheless the best of his pre-war films, with an organisation of movement and direction of actors — particularly in the trial scenes — which sometimes looks forward to *Beyond a Reasonable Doubt*. And most notably of all, the superb *Secret Beyond the Door* preceded *Clash by Night* by three years, thus giving one the sense of witnessing a curious lowering of both sights and tone, an incomprehensible contraction in Lang's viewpoint. In fact, Lang was never again to reach quite these heights except in *Beyond a Reasonable Doubt* and the two parts of *The Tiger of Eschnapur*. So Lang's climactic period began in 1948 with a *mise en scène* which ceased being a prop for the script or a superficial decoration of space to become intense and inward, calling people and settings into question, predicated upon such fundamental problems as eyes, hand movements, the sudden illumination of abysses. Here the script supports the *mise en scène*, which becomes the end. Which explains why this period is also the one which was to see Lang abandoned by people who see *mise en scène* as a certain way of padding out a story on the screen, or a spectacular and meaningless visual display powerless to attain the essence.

*   *   *

The heights I mentioned, the distinctively Langian tone which derives from an eagle eye under which everything achieves parity, attest to a cosmic sense latent throughout the last films and suddenly erupting in the final shots of *The Tiger of Eschnapur*, where it is incarnated, even symbolised, by the hallucinatory gesture of the fugitive discharging his weapon at the sun. Psychological and moral motives are resorbed, transcended; events embark at once on the terrain of man's relationship to the world, this world which he does not own. Here we have pure tragedy: not some paltry criticism of mankind, but a description of fate. The best way to demonstrate this elevation in tone is by comparing *Clash by Night, Human Desire* and *The Tiger of Eschnapur*. The same situation — the 'eternal triangle', as Lang himself puts it, in which a man loves a woman who loves another man and rejects the first — occasions three *mises en scène*, the first remaining at ground level and becoming bogged down in little psychological ruts dug by the script, the second undergoing rather more decantation, while the perfectly crystalline third shimmers with love and hatred in their purest state, being no more than a linear account of the acts whereby these raw and heightened passions are brought into the world, acts whose incandescence consumes, obliterates even the characters themselves, liberating passion from all fetters and thus investing it, in its widest sense, with the most haunting poignancy. Lang's films, freed from the need to express ideas through an articulation of incident, become insignificant narratives whose significance is contained in the *mise en scène*: this meaning is purely emotional, and so purely aesthetic, no longer conceptual but melodic, with the result that Lang is one of that rare band of film-makers in whose hands the cinema achieves the dignity of art.

Gone are themes, 'directorial touches', characters, and can one still talk of life? Nothing is left but a sort of line which one watches as it advances and finally overtakes itself again. The actors are plunged into a neutral zone now illuminated only by the secret depths of their relationships forged by the stark impulse of an ineluctable momentum. Each situation is merely a moment in this progress, and extinguishes

14

itself in the next moment: the film destroys itself as it evolves, effacing its trail behind it. Each element is indispensable to the whole without existing in its own right. With Lang, there is no dominant viewpoint. The *mise en scène*, in the most etymological sense of the phrase, becomes an end in itself and its mechanism infallibly grinds down everything that serves its function: the gestures, faces, voices and settings impress us less for what they are than for what they become, and more precisely for the ineluctable form of this development. It is worth noting in passing that abstraction like this finds colour a hindrance, or at least a superfluous element, and gravitates towards black-and-white which reveals the essential directly 'without embarking on the indirections, however dazzling, of concrete realism. So the colour in *The Tiger of Eschnapur* and *The Indian Tomb* is admirable because, unlike the warm colours that dazzle in American films (well suited to more sensual film-makers like Losey or Don Weis), it glows with a muted brilliance which sustains rather than contradicts this entirely limpid universe in its delicately discriminating restraint.

So the fascination sought from the outset is achieved, by interiorising the mathematical design, which no longer distorts appearances but selects and arranges them on an emotional substratum. The problem here is to exorcise certain obsessions by subjecting them to such control through calculation, abstraction, summation, that they become inhuman; to reduce an existential problem to a theorem, in other words, in order to dominate and control it. The problem is to objectify these obsessions, to wrench oneself free of them and forget oneself while watching them live independently, to establish a distance of silence and lucidity between oneself and them. The problem, finally, is to achieve, through a fanatical domination of the content, a harmony such that the intolerable can be circumscribed within it and made acceptable, even welcome. The moments of horror (especially in *Secret Beyond the Door, While the City Sleeps, Moonfleet* and *The Tiger of Eschnapur*) plunge the human being into the impasse of a totally hostile environment — which brings us to a consideration of the role of the settings in Lang's work. Following the German tradition, these settings, unless effaced by the same impulse towards abstraction as the physical presence of the actors (most notably in *Beyond a Reasonable Doubt*), function within a purely dramatic perspective, charged with malevolent power, with *angst* (tentatively expressed, and symbolised by, the famous clocks of the primitive period), massive, opaque architectural structures whose mystery (the sense of impending collapse) or power to envelop, to stifle, to terrify, is accentuated by their nudity once the drama has opened up its abyss.

Hatred, premeditated murder, and a bleak eroticism doomed to disaster comprise a universe of implacable hostility, of glacial encounters, in which the only alternative is: hunt or be hunted. Here, following a dialectic whose rigour is worthy of Hegel, each consciousness desires the death of another. The recurring pretexts for this *mise en scène* — personal vengeance, legal punishment, collective persecution — are so many jungle disguises, or ideal grounds for the suppression of the unacceptable *other*. The Langian shot *par excellence* is the one in which the executioner contemplates his victim, establishing him as an object, in a sort of implacable possession by remote control suggestive of the spider and the fly relationship. (In this Fuller coincides with Lang, though more given to embroidery.) The bodies are seized by a paralysis which restricts their movements within an almost fixed frame. The faces are closed, impassive not only in reticence but because the world is already dead, petrified, each individual being imprisoned without recourse, therefore devoid of anguish, beyond solitude, dispatched purely because of the bond of antagonism, indifference or contempt. Carnal relationships are of the same icy nature, tricked out with a facade of attraction, empoisoned by repulsion, attempts to violate frigid flesh, or simply epidermal coupling without awareness. The actresses are cool, like Joan Fontaine and Sally Forrest, or decked out to excite an old man's fancy (Ida Lupino, Rhonda Fleming, Barbara Nichols). Even in *The Tiger of Eschnapur,* where the woman for once is allowed her full sensual seductiveness, her body offering its firm, sombre weight in voluptuous movements, a sinuous living bronze flushed with blood, she is really only presenting her prince with a version of the torments of Tantalus in which, surrounded by perils, are compounded the desire, the object and the obstacle which are to explode in a long, mute cry of helplessness and hatred. Only after this will serenity be possible.

But this approach to a physical presence is exceptional in Lang's work. Whereas Joseph Losey, sharing many of the same concerns, seeks and exhausts the actor's potentialities through an almost tangible proximity, Lang — rejecting an infinity of possibilities — effaces him to the point of effacing the very texture of his narrative. Lang's universe is irremediable. As with all great, bleak works of art, the paradox of Lang's films is that they fascinate us with their dark spells, their unholy delight in a tragic system, their contemplation of the inhuman. Exaltation is born here of the destruction of all hope, with man imprisoning himself within a fatality against which he turns the closed mask of his contempt. A reversal is thus effected within the very confines of negation, which turns itself inside out like a pelt to show its other face of victory; the contradiction is an affirmation on behalf of the defeated; man as Pascal saw him, greater than that which oppresses him.

Beyond a Reasonable Doubt, and even more particularly *The Tiger of Eschnapur* and *The Indian Tomb,* mark the limits beyond which *mise en scène,* by a process analogous to Mallarmé's, would tip over into an absence of *mise en scène.* Any further domination of the content would result in its suppression, and would lie beyond the mediating role of art. This mania

16

for perfection, for an autocratic art through which the creator attempts to screen the most precious part of himself from chance, pushes Lang's method to extremes of audibility and credibility. Which is why he is so little heard and so little believed.

(Translated by Tom Milne)

PHILIPPE DEMONSABLON

The Imperious Dialectic of Fritz Lang

(*Originally published in* Cahiers du Cinéma, *no. 99, September 1959*)

> His solar eagle's eye, his particular sensitivity, had persuaded him once and for all that the only certainty we may have of tomorrow's reality lies in pessimism, that ultimate form of the solitude to which we come for recuperation, admonition and rest. — René Char.

If one had to prove that Fritz Lang's work owes much to premeditation and very little to accidents that may be seen as either happy or unhappy depending upon circumstances, one could find a rich harvest of arguments simply by making a close study of the scripts for his films. It is in fact no secret that even in those cases where he was not personally producing subjects close to his heart, Lang — himself a former screenwriter — usually had the projects that were offered to him reworked under his supervision. So let us start by granting the responsibility he has for the themes of these films; we can take off from them to make a first contact with an *auteur* in whom continuity of thought is more important than the obvious and requisite evolution of a style.

Concerted over more than thirty years, his *oeuvre* has made contrasting motifs echo within its confines: manhunt and vengeance, innocence and defiance, fascination and freedom, obsessional solitude and no less an obsession with promiscuity. Emerging from this we can see not only the persistence of certain themes but also their diversity, and above all, evidence of a continuous movement whereby these differences, finding their proper role, merge together though without any attendant loss in definition. As with any *oeuvre*, Lang's develops not like a syllogism but like a tree. It structures itself as it grows. It produces its principles as it takes form, and never ceases modifying itself as it becomes more deeply committed to existence. So the presence of a theme, no matter how well attested, is really less important to the overall system than this circuit during which it develops, digs deeper, modifies, changes direction. It is in contradictions and reversals that Lang's imagination finds its most powerful stimulus, and each of his films invariably arrives at a particular point where, under the accumulation of contraries, it can no longer proceed except as a result of its own disequilibrium: the most urgent sense of creation is expressed by the dialectical movement. The very

18

words which spring to mind to describe particular films — defeat, oppression, pursuit, defiance, revenge — are associated with essentially dynamic ideas. It is this dynamism which I would like to examine first in certain specific instances which anyone familiar with Lang's work will know to be exemplary.

M (1932) brings off the difficult task of presenting a totally opaque character, familiarity with whom can only deepen the mystery. As revealed to us, his actions, expressions and gestures remain alien, situating him in a fundamentally *other* world. Eyes unaware of the impulses behind them, movements uncertain of their destination: the Broderick Crawford character in *Human Desire* (1954) is an extension of Peter Lorre's *M*. The touch of inconsequence would doubtless suggest a behaviourist aesthetic in this imposture which is so effective in alienating what remains familiar or accessible to us, except that here the imposture would have been in venturing to offer the slightest explanation, in making the least approach. *Noli me tangere*: do not touch me, for I am other. The greatness of Fritz Lang is always apparent in what he refuses to do; and any approach here would remain partial, as would any social or psychoanalytical explanation. Partial, and all the more illusory in regard to audiences only too ready to be satisfied. 'Why does this man kill?' the recent remake of *M* asks. 'It doesn't matter,' Lang had already replied, and the last shot movingly confirms this, 'it doesn't matter since he has killed; ask rather why this sort of man exists.' Guilt, innocence: gradually we see these notions dissolve, overtaken by a mind advancing to confront and ponder them.

Expressionism, even interpreted in the light of Lang's personal requirements, played a very small part in this triumph: in fact, no stylistic rupture accompanied his removal to America, yet ten years were to pass before Lang recaptured this purity of movement. In his first transatlantic films, plot was to take precedence over what one might call, after Rohmer and Chabrol, 'the formal postulate'. The themes emerge more systematically, not without leaving a certain sense of provocation. The rise to power of Nazism can only have made Lang increasingly aware of the viciousness of mob enthusiasms: this may indeed be the inspiration behind the false Maria's rabble-rousing of the masses in *Metropolis* (1926). Driven out of Germany by Nazism, Lang was to turn for a time to highly aggressive forms of individual affirmation in the face of collective pressures. This was pre-eminently the period of antisocial characters, of the hero who was by turn victim and avenger. In *Fury* (1936), a man accused of a crime he did not commit is nearly lynched by the mob who burn down the jail; escaping unbeknown to anyone, he lets the trial of his assassins proceed, and they reveal themselves to be as contemptible individually as they were in a group.

You Only Live Once (1937) again interweaves the notions of innocence and guilt, not this time in order to transcend them through the

19

confrontation, but rather to counterpoint them in a fugal development. The hero's position with regard to society is always one beat ahead — or behind — the notion society forms of that position. When he is innocent, it claims he is guilty; he becomes guilty just as (other things being equal . . . but the nature of things is to change) his innocence is about to be established. Man at grips with the shifting hazards of life: is Lang at one with Hawks in this respect? No, because we can see at once how Lang differs, heightening the contrasts which Hawks reconciles, stressing the ridges where Hawks maintains a harmonious curve. Hawks reveals a desire to show man consonant with the world; Lang insists on the irremediable antagonism between them.

Yet we are still a long way from the pessimism of *The Blue Gardenia* (1952), which was to be attained by way of the series of weak and despicable characters inaugurated by *The Woman in the Window* (1944). Here, spurning all verisimilitude, Lang undertook the description of a world which, as the dream stresses, is not so much imaginary as entirely possible. A world too facilely described as one of fatality: for where does destiny come in if the character expends the little liberty he has on his own downfall, and where the inexorable decree in this play of forces which he retains the privilege of setting in motion if not always of controlling? This kind of destiny cannot be fulfilled without the co-operation of the victim (even back in the days of *M*, the little girls at the beginning offered themselves to a potential murderer by singing about his exploits), and no matter how perfect the circle encompassing him, it cannot close in unless he consents. Everything here tends to present him as the only anomaly, the only obtrusive element in this world: were he not to intervene, cause and effect would maintain themselves in loose symmetry, and only his desire to act disturbs the balance. Lang often delights in endowing even the most *natural* gesture with repercussions so weighty that the mind, powerless to deny the patent fact, finds itself questioning the logical system behind it: Edward G. Robinson's finger marking the exact spot on Joan Bennett's back where he will later stab her with an ice-pick,[1] Marlene Dietrich being mortally wounded precisely where she wore the jewel which was torn from her;[2] acts are constantly being attracted to the channels dug for them. Similarly with the idea that governs *The Woman in the Window*, an idea so fascinating that it would pass unnoticed but for the sense of vertigo it instils in the spectator: that all relationships of causality are operating *backwards* here — in other words, as if they were in fact operating in the creator's imagination since, in realising a particular image which he has in mind, he arranges the causes with a view to the

1. *Scarlet Street* (1945).
2. *Rancho Notorious* (1951). This jewel had been stolen from the murdered girl. Thus the two women are doubly equated in death: the ideas behind Lang's *mise en scène* are always over-determined — hence their beauty.

effect he wants to obtain. The power of this film derives from the fact that it assigns to the domain of *reality* what belongs to the domain of *fiction*: it is by realising with maximum objectivity the demiurgic dream natural to any artist that Lang surmounts the contradictions inherent in the formal postulate. At this point in our analysis it is not impermissible to see *The Woman in the Window* as a first draft for *Beyond a Reasonable Doubt* (1956). Undoubtedly the second version is more perfectly realised, with the dialectical movement entirely manifest in the work itself rather than merely in meditation on it; but it should be noted here that in both cases the contradictions are put forward simply as so many obstacles inviting the mind to renewed activity, and the paradox, far from offering itself as definitive, serves merely as a stimulus.

For Lang — and we shall see other examples of this — delights in choosing the most extreme form of obstacle, so that the mind cannot entertain it except under a tension which obviates any placidity. Whatever he is expressing, it does not seem to occur to him to do it in any other way than through this agitation which, as with the potion of which a philosopher remarked that it 'decomposed if it is not stirred', is necessary to the life of any thought. And there would be little point in referring to Heraclitus if Fritz Lang's work did not claim such obvious kinship with the man who made of 'conflict the father and supreme ruler of all things'. In it, the will plays a prominent role; not so much for its victories or defeats as for the contact it attempts to establish between man and the world through these victories and defeats. The Lang hero questions the world by listening to the repercussions his acts evoke within it; his movements submit, in order to reveal them, to the forces which govern them; and the motive he thus seeks is none other than his own. Although usually operating to the detriment of man, whose liberty it thwarts, this solidarity with the world is evoked time and again:[3] with unfailing persistence, Lang has his characters surrender to scenes of rest and relaxation, sometimes lengthy and often effusive, before leaving them prey to their most terrible trials. A favourite ploy for poets and moralists, you may say, citing a hundred and one examples of this sort of transient happiness. No doubt, but Lang does not make it a subject for pity, however moving, nor yet an appeal to stoicism, however exalted. Consider, rather, the birthday dinner which Anne Baxter treats herself to in *The Blue Gardenia*, an interlude sparing no detail of ritual, a remission of the malice which is fully revealed only subsequently: a concern for construction may not be entirely irrelevant to a vacillation like this (the harder the fall will be), but the construction itself is primarily devoted to the reminder that destiny is invariably the product of man's weakness — as though man, in the dialogue with the world which constitutes the compulsive form of his actions, could not relax his

3. To cite Heraclitus again: 'The common law is universal; but although this law determines the universe, most act as though intelligence has its own laws.'

will for a moment without finding the equilibrium around him shattered.

And where movement satisfies an imperious need, sheer immobility is intolerable. Lang creates almost tangible images to bring out this horror. In *The Woman in the Window* there is the corpse momentarily standing up, as though alive. Or in *Rancho Notorious*, the mouth unable to utter a sound, the mouth of the killer whose life Arthur Kennedy promises to spare *as long as he can shout*. Or the accused in *Fury*, and their panic impulse to efface the image when they see themselves in court *suspended* in the act of their crime as the amateur film is frozen from time to time to identify each of them in turn. No frame still from the film can convey the sense of horror felt by the spectator at this moment, and which would be less overwhelming if it did not suggest the idea of a violence committed against nature.

The fact that a feeling like this can still develop suffices to show that all life is not excluded from this system, however glacial its reflections and however sharp its edges. Maybe (and one can't be sure, after all) humanism is no longer valid when one has to make such bitter comparison between the human and inhuman. Yet, even imprisoned within this dialectical necessity whose characteristics I have outlined, tenderness and pliability still earn some attention for their own sake. Lang, as I said, sometimes allows his characters to soften and the tension of their wills to slacken; but for him this is also the moment to relax the tension of his thought, to let it seek respite from the concept with the object it caresses and which nourishes it. So scenes of contemplation and repose abound, usually favouring the female characters. With her muted flexibility, Sylvia Sidney was destined, like Brigitte Helm, to incarnate precarious, imperilled charm, and *Fury* reveals the depth of her gentle tenacity; *You Only Live Once* equates her with Gretchen, making her instinctively exalted, inflicting searching torments only to see her serenity grow. But it was left to Joan Bennett to achieve the miracle of sovereign beauty. Just watch her make the light with which she is invested in *The Woman in the Window* shimmer with an inner palpitation, a peerless subject for a great sculptor and the only source of warmth within the film's stern geometry. A somewhat schematic abstraction? Then watch her execute the most astonishing gestures imagined by a film-maker in *Scarlet Street*, consider the pose prescribed by Lang as she stretches out on a sofa to write a letter on the floor below her, or the one with which she pokes a foot from beneath her dress; even that very finger I have already mentioned lingers to celebrate the supple pliability of this body. *Cloak and Dagger* (1946) devotes the same tender attention to Lilli Palmer's sleeping form. There is, however, nothing sensual about these moments of pure abeyance which one so distinctly feels to be turned towards some *elsewhere*: 'While I await my thought, it is only proper that my eyes should be occupied with some particularly propitious object,'

declared a Faust whom Lang would not have rejected: the Faust of Paul
Valéry . . .

*   *   *

Creative maturity was to reject these casual charms which the mature
man had not disdained. The beauty celebrated hitherto was to be
successively disparaged, banished, and finally ignored: the mutation
Gloria Grahame suffers between *The Big Heat* and *Human Desire* is a fairly
eloquent example — although this is only a beginning and one of the
more obvious signs. Over the past few years we have seen Lang
gradually strip his films of all seduction for the eye, then for the heart and
the more venal aspects of the mind, nevertheless sacrificing nothing of
the ideal figure that haunts him. And if an occasional shot unexpectedly
lets us glimpse Joan Bennett through Barbara Stanwyck, or Glenn Ford
in Arthur Franz, it is through these tangential moments that the ideal
figure manifests its presence; but I am only too well aware that we must
go much further in order to define its contours, however difficult it may
be to follow the progress of an idea when one has simply come under its
spell.

For here the pleasures of sight and sound do not equate with the
expressive purpose. Fritz Lang's *oeuvre* takes its stance under the sign of
the idea, and in his films it is always the idea we perceive in guises that
derive from pure *mise en scène*: here spirit and matter put each other to the
trial, and in this interchange the visual elements converge with the idea
which justifies them, so that the film maintains a dual existence, finally
existing only through this duality. There is, however, no question of
illustrating the idea (as if a masquerade could render it more accessible!), but rather of testing its power; and what would this power be if the
idea did not prove itself capable of giving form to matter, of subjecting it
to authoritative creation by organising it? But once the screening is over,
who notices all these self-imposed difficulties conquered in silence, the
perfection of the match-cutting on movement, the precision of gesture
and grouping? The economy Lang achieves here, totally without
compromise, shows that for him these are only means — or passageways
— to an end, and not elements in a technique glorified for its own power
or perfection.

But the virtues of the figure are *also* those of the idea that inspired it: in
this harmony lies the unresolved enigma of the unexplained beauty of the
films. Perfection and finish correspond to a strict necessity: nothing but
what was conjured may be permitted entry here (and if Lang has earned
a reputation as an architect-builder, it is because he refuses to leave
anything to chance), no gesture, no movement, no glance may be
expressed differently from what we are shown. Even the very least touch

in the direction becomes the mark of such necessity that the entire film seems permeated by signs, and even what is natural becomes too natural. Imperiously, a zone of light traces a path within the fixity of a shot, an angle in the decor directs the eye, some mysterious curvature in space induces the actors' movements. The least touch, I repeat: in *The Big Heat* (1953), for instance, a long interior scene between Glenn Ford and Jocelyn Brando is shot entirely from angles directed towards the centre of the room; and it is left to a totally innocuous shot, a reverse angle, to show her with her back to the window because the explosion which kills her a few minutes later is to be similarly framed. Signs like this abound in Lang's work, and not merely in the espionage films which for many years presented him with a perfect excuse to make extensive use of them without ever revealing the cipher. The tone of cruelty and anguish sanctioned by the genre at least ensured that Lang was able to fulfil a long-cherished plan: to grant the characters awareness only of their acts, after having withdrawn from them all awareness of the forces determining them — the latter devolving instead upon the spectator so as to evoke the sense of tragic horror in him. Once established, this was to remain so.

Because there would be no point in subjecting his actors to the forces of light and objects, no point in breaking them to the laws of geometry, unless to direct attention beyond the characters. Human, too human . . . if attention is fixed on the characters, how can it attain the idea? Out of wonder, thought must be born: the film's task is to describe a labyrinth, not to deliver its secret, which is none of its concern. If, as Goethe believed, art consists in masking with a mantle the figure whose living image the artist carries within him, then what we see is Lang weaving an ever lighter garment over nerves that are increasingly taut. Meanwhile the signs progressively lose their mystery and merge with the idea itself. The decor becomes airier — but also arid; the light becomes uniform — but also implacable. The few anecdotal elements remaining now disappear, and the necessity increases accordingly. *Rancho Notorious* and *Moonfleet* (1954) are simply two romantic flares, two way stations where the eye (if not the heart) may warm itself on this journey into austerity begun with *Clash by Night* (1951) — an austerity placed at the service of a wider idea rather than retailing truths about specimens of humanity, who are on the contrary laminated, polished, calibrated. Earlier, of course, Lang had already found a way to dehumanise actors within the decorative pretext for *Die Nibelungen* (1923-4); and he returned to the attack more vigorously, not now attempting to give his actors any semblance of abstraction. Because of its realism, *The Blue Gardenia* is able to treat its characters with methodical contempt; and in this leave-taking from them, the corrosive touch was doubtless essential for once: an etching, after all, is revealed by the acid which eats away its surface. But Lang went further yet; and the larval existence that falls to the lot of the

24

actors in *Clash by Night*, and especially *Human Desire*, strikes an even severer blow against the notion of character. Here they act like somnambulists, and their behaviour, in defiance of any psychology, invites a correspondingly sharper delineation. The opacity here cannot mask a dazzling trenchancy: lightning shines brightest in the dark, and of its own accord the idea, reduced to its own self, inexorably proceeds, freed from any consciousness likely to absorb it.

Are these films to be reproached for exciting only basic feelings? It is obvious that what is at issue here can only be a *scrutiny* of man. Dolly back, and the actor advances obliquely; pan, and he squeezes between a wall and the impassive eye of the camera; dolly forward, and he retreats humbled before that eye . . . a movement so often misused in other films, but here pregnant with unspoken things. Towards the end of his life, a man contemplates without passion his experience of men; he maintains a necessary distance, placing his faith and his consolation in pessimism. Is this the ultimate secret? No, and Lang once again comes full circle: for no matter how schematic his characters may have become, no matter how close they come to being pure ideas, they are *thereby* also brought closer to the spectator. This unblinking eye, this merciless gaze directed on the simulacra which occupy the screen . . . suddenly the spectator feels it turned on him, reflecting this scarcely flattering portrait of himself. Why accept it, you may say. Because no one is exempt from intelligence — and yet, in the light of intelligence alone, no one is spared.

(Translated by Tom Milne)

RAYMOND BELLOUR

On Fritz Lang

This article first appeared in Critique *no. 226 (March 1966), and was reprinted in the collection of essays and interviews by Bellour entitled* Le Livre des Autres *(Paris, L'Herne 1971).*

In the first part of the article Bellour examines the totality of discourses (films, criticism, biography of Lang, statements by Lang) which have so far produced the space in (particularly French) film culture which bears the director's name. It is thus a useful example of a kind of 'second-generation' auteurism, working at a distance, at a remove, approaching the individual film-texts indirectly, through the other texts which have accrued to them. In particular, Bellour is attempting to account for the special fascination worked by the Lang-text on earlier French auteurist critics like Mourlet and Demonsablon, a fascination so acute and obsessive that it produced the sort of Romantic excesses so apparent in the preceding two articles (Lang's 'eagle eye' and 'cosmic sense', etc). His 'solution' centres on what he calls the 'primacy of vision' in Lang's work, and the subsequent examination of particular elements of Lang's adored mise en scène *constitutes an attempt to discover what 'lies beneath this word "vision", how exactly Lang endows it with force . . . in what form it shows or shows through'.*

In a sense the article ties in with Peter Wollen's 'revised version' of la politique des auteurs, *whereby the director (the person) is distinguished from (or, as here, opposed to) the structure named after him or her, in that Bellour insists on the need for close examination of formal devices because it is questions of form which are repressed from the person Lang's discourse. But Bellour has subsequently stressed, in both articles (e.g., 'Hitchcock the Enunciator' in* Camera Obscura *2) and interview (*Camera Obscura *3/4), the importance he attaches to the idea of enunciation in film: 'What I'm trying to do by insisting on enunciation is to show that a certain subject is speaking under certain conditions in particular films. This logic of enunciation can more or less correspond to the category designated by the name and the work of an author (it certainly corresponds perfectly in the case of Hitchcock and Lang).' He states that this logic 'can also apply much more generally to a genre or to the production of a given company at a specific moment in their history', but also stresses that textual analysis, the critical activity with which he is primarily associated, 'both specifies and revitalises the question raised by* Cahiers du Cinéma *under the heading of* la politique des auteurs'. *The crucial step forward from simple, 'innocent' auteurism is that he views the place of enunciation ('the place at once productive and empty of the subject-director') as 'the place of a certain subject of discourse and consequently of a certain subject of desire' (as opposed, essentially, to* *the subject of a world-view). And this leads Bellour directly to 'the problem which I can see has been more and more important in my own work: the problem of the status of woman and of the masculine subject who defines himself in relation to her, both in the classical cinema and in classical narrative'. That this is the area which lies just outside the parameters of this article is indicated by the remark that with the Lang-text, 'One feels effort, the temptation of the possible, the distance between desire and its object'. The significance of this 'hint' emerges ten years later when Bellour writes of 'the function and purpose of a certain kind of cinema of representation which privileges in the enunciation apparatus the object of desire . . . For the man-subject who is behind the camera, this image of fear or pleasure which is delegated to the woman as other, this image is the condition necessary to the constitution of his phantasy. Here, Hitchcock the enunciator'. Here, Lang . . .*

Enmeshed in paradox, Fritz Lang's destiny is an astonishing one.

Like Stroheim, though not an actor invested with the high prestige attendant upon any abused genius, like Sternberg, though never associated with any woman like Marlene, like Murnau, who died a death shrouded in mystery forty long years ago, Fritz Lang was one of the first to become enshrined in cinematic legend; and the first, in a sense, to achieve this in his lifetime and purely as a film-maker. There is Welles, of course: once again an actor whose fame — in myth, at least — rests on his hoaxing of America. And there is Hitchcock. But the myth is rather too heavily disguised by the image-making, the sociological phenomenon which conceals the essence. Lang alone, in a sense, incarnates the notion of *mise en scène* quite so decisively or so abstractly. Not that his life is irrelevant to this image. His non-compliance with Goebbels, his flight from Germany and disenchanted return after twenty years of exile in America, the way in which he set himself up, from *Siegfried* onwards, as the film-maker of destiny, all this lends Lang an explosive density. This is the horizon which nurtures the pure, rigorous image of cinema in the highest sense of the word.

In 1922, after *Der müde Tod,* Lang was generally acknowledged to be an important film-maker, the most important in Germany along with Murnau. Twelve years later, he was in Hollywood. Caught in the toils of the American machine, he made twenty-three films, a little more than one a year. He filmed everything that could be filmed in Hollywood, even though often exercising choice and turning down projects: psychological and social dramas, thrillers, war films, adventure films, Westerns, with *You and Me* fringing on the only two missing categories, comedy and the musical. Lang became a Hollywood director; against his will, the creator of *Metropolis* did a remake of *La Bête humaine.* He was considered a great director, praised for his exceptional austerity and incisiveness. No more

27

than that. The greatness of Hollywood lies largely in the lack of critical distance.

But when Lang left America in 1958, an idea had already begun to take shape in France. For Astruc, Rivette, Rohmer or Douchet, Lang was no longer a film-maker quite like the rest. Not that he was more important; the problem lay elsewhere: Lang, in a sense, embodied the specific property of cinema, what was described in a term rife with ambiguities as '*mise en scène*'. Through the double game played by his American and German films, a remarkable continuity is revealed, more or less explicit, becoming increasingly rigorous. The paradox of Lang's American films, buttressed as they are by their German synonyms, is this: they show, in the strict sense of the word, how what one must loosely describe as a vision of the world, unequivocally displayed earlier in Lang's German films, takes shape through the more pragmatic view. So, in his own way and as if in comparison, he accords pride of place to viewpoint; and it is no accident that, from *Fury* onwards, both in his images and in the implications of his scripts, the focus of Lang's *mise en scène* is so often vision itself, articulated in various ways among which the most obvious is the presence of the investigator, the reporter or the photographer, the man who sees and seizes appearances within the rectangular frame of his camera.

Every film-maker, in a sense, defines the essence of cinema, but is there another for whom it is so nakedly, and so unequivocally, as with Lang, the ultimate metaphor? When a Sternberg film reveals the potential of vision, and one seeks the point of focus, one is instantly thrown back on Woman, the object and subject of perception. In the case of Hitchcock, over and above a moral system bound up with appearances, one is thrown back on a vertiginous reduplication of the symbolic duality of the theme. In the case of Eisenstein, on the visual and dramatic feasibility of a historical dialectic. With Lang, however, what else can one say but a vision of vision? This does not imply a pointless duplication in which Lang's art fritters itself away, enmeshed in its own myth; on the contrary, it broadens the horizon in all directions, and validates Lang's answer to the question 'What is the most indispensable quality for a film-maker?': 'He must know life'. Life, here, should be understood as the locus within which vision is exercised. There remains the question of what lies behind this word vision, exactly what power Lang invests it with, and in what form it appears, tangibly or intangibly.

Herein lies the explanation for the enthusiasm, inexplicable to some, of certain Lang admirers for his last three films. Filmed in Germany, using a theme and stories from his early period, by a man made master of fiction in all its guises by his American experience, *The 1000 Eyes of Dr Mabuse*, *The Tiger of Eschnapur* and *The Indian Tomb* present the paradox of being at once remarkably veiled and disconcertingly open. Seemingly naive, almost puerile — particularly in the case of the Indian diptych,

28

since a certain grave urgency of theme may be glimpsed beneath the serial conventions and inconsequence of the last *Mabuse* film — these films, theoretical in the extreme, discard the reassuring alibi of the American tradition while simultaneously transposing the tradition's basic artificiality to a Germany where nothing has survived: they repudiate the positive aspects of the myths underlying Lang's German period, reducing them to their own level within a dual adventure, individual and collective, involving the cinema and historical awareness. With exceptional integrity, this destructive-reflective irony of Lang's toys with the hackneyed stories placed at his disposal, seemingly in derisory fidelity to himself, but in his third *Mabuse* disrupting the final ploys of vision and of life, immersing the myth in reflections which bring it face to face with its ultimate reality: the cinema as what it might be, metaphorically revealed not only in the symbolic title, *The 1000 Eyes*, but in the dazzling visual reduplication of the television screens which Mabuse, reincarnated in his son — and more particularly, one might say, as has of course been said, in the film-maker himself— has at his disposal in the foyer of the Hotel Luxor. As for the two Indian films, dazzling moments flitting through precariousness, they tell only of a fine and judicious persistence in which despair surfaces, in which the *mise en scène*, and even the very idea of *mise en scène*, looms, as Blanchot said of writing, in the silence that envelops it, a sundering of the elements which compose it, an inability to lie carried to the point of tragedy.

So it is not surprising that, from the point of view of the myth, these films — which may be the last in one of the few bodies of work stretching over nearly fifty years of film-making — constitute a vital document. For today, with Fritz Lang entering legend in France, far from America which never really fathomed him, and from his native Germany which was unable to reclaim him, the audiences flocking to the Cinémathèque are coming more or less consciously to admire the man who, in his work, has envisaged film as the ultimate metaphor, and whom Godard's inspired casting plunged into the two-faced game of *Le Mépris*. Lang observes the brilliantly coloured statues of Greek legend, his only assets, just as the gardens, the palaces and the actors he was entrusted with were in *The Indian Tomb*, like vast marionettes around which beauty bloomed. Held in contempt by the producer who pays him, contemptuous of everything which is not life and this power to express it inherent in vision, alone, disenchanted but determined to preserve truth in and around himself, Lang endlessly films *The Odyssey*, telling of life already caught in the toils of its own fiction.

So Lang plays a subtle and skilful game with his subjects, with each component of his work, an authoritative, more or less veiled game which demands to be lucidly formulated through the forty films he has made. He himself, as one might expect, offers little help. In the fine, entirely documentary book edited by Alfred Eibel,[1] Lang indulges and con-

1. *Présence du Cinéma*, 1964.

tradicts himself, limiting his remarks to matters of plot and conception, to the thematic, political and social aspects of each of his films, or else taking what looks like ironical refuge in comments about technique. But the testimony of his various collaborators invites, albeit allusively, consideration of the question of a form which Lang always pretends to be unaware of. For all of them, actors, scriptwriters, cameramen, art directors, paint a portrait of an extraordinarily meticulous man, attentive to the slightest gesture, demanding of each image a precise life which constantly challenges the deceptive banality of the narrative. Out of this volume of scattered, fascinating fragments which follows in its subject's tracks, illuminating and bringing him into focus, comes the certainty that the more Lang insists on the apparent meaning of his films, the more the enigma of this meaning must be resolved by a systematic examination of the form whose multiple articulations may be sensed in the films, and only in the clear light of which may the irreducible impression of a totality be maintained.

It may seem surprising that no critic has as yet succeeded in being totally illuminating[2] about a film-maker so radically bound up with the essence of his art, as for instance Claude Ollier was in his brilliant article on Sternberg,[3] even though dealing with only one film; and that no one, in considering the infinite diversity and rigour of Lang's films, has attempted to define the paradoxes and the curious fractured unity which emerges throughout Alfred Eibel's book and in Lang's recent confession, so rich in tone with reverberations, ambiguities and provocation, which in memory of his native city he has titled, 'La nuit viennoise.'[4]

My purpose here is merely to assemble, in a semi-haphazard way, a few of the many elements which, when described, analysed in detail, classified according to the connections they establish, would serve as a basis for a systematic approach to the Langian universe. Notes, in a sense, for a cinemanalysis.

2. Worthy of mention, however, are Lotte Eisner's unfortunately too brief article ('Notes sur le style de Fritz Lang', *Revue du Cinéma* no. 5, February 1947) and the relevant pages in her *The Haunted Screen*, which, it is to be hoped, are merely the prelude to a more general study to come. There are also articles by Gérard Legrand ('Notes pour un éloge de Fritz Lang', *Positif* nos. 50-51-52, March 1963) and Michel Mourlet ('Trajectoire de Fritz Lang' in *Sur un art ignoré*, La Table Ronde, 1965). Above all, there are remarkable articles by Jacques Rivette on *Beyond a Reasonable Doubt* ('La main', *Cahiers du Cinéma* no. 76, November 1957), Jean-Luc Godard on *The Return of Frank James* (Ufoleis *fiche*, 1955) and Jean Douchet on *The 1000 Eyes of Dr Mabuse* ('L'étrange obsession', *Cahiers du Cinéma* no. 122, August 1961).

3. Claude Ollier, 'Une aventure de la lumière', *Cahiers du Cinéma* no. 168, July 1965.

4. *Cahiers du Cinéma* no. 169, August 1965.

1. A film-maker's position is defined by the relationship he establishes with his characters. In a film, one of the forms of this relationship depends on the systems of vision revealed by the images: how does the film-maker indicate and incorporate the fragmental[5] viewpoint of his characters within the continuity of his own viewpoint, in other words the viewpoint of the film. Minnelli, for example, generally remains outside the conspectus he is describing; Hitchcock, on the contrary, uses the clearly defined viewpoints of his characters within the scheme of his own vision. But in this respect Lang displays, crucially, a disturbing ambiguity.

There is a strictly unequivocal way of defining a character's viewpoint: sandwiching a shot of the object seen between two identical shots of the person seeing it. Often Lang indicates this certainty as a possibility, only instantly to deny it and plunge into equivocality. For example, three *looks* by the killer in *While the City Sleeps*.

— During the first murder, he is framed waist upwards in front of the door: we feel that he is indeed looking at something, but we don't know what; there follows a very brief close-up, of the latch on the door; but the following shot has no connection with his scrutiny.

— The killer enters Dorothy Kyne's studio: in a mirror he sees her straightening her stocking with a slow, caressing gesture; the close shot that follows, showing the killer in the middle of the room, offers no confirmation as to what he presumably saw.

— Later he leaves the house and moves toward a low window giving on to the bar; he bends down, and we see the bar in long shot; the camera is outside, as the distortion of the glass confirms; everything implies that the image represents exactly what the killer is seeing, but since Lang cuts away to something else instead of returning to the killer, there is no proof that this is so.

In different ways, through these three forms of reticence, Lang lets ambiguity hover over the relationship which unites character and creator through viewpoint. Almost all his films reveal this same attitude. It is absolutely manifest, for instance, in the sequence with the lepers, repeated in both *The Tiger of Eschnapur* and *The Indian Tomb*. And Lang plays on it deliberately in *The Blue Gardenia*, where Norah's return to consciousness entails distorted images, again leaving two possibilities to be confronted: either Lang is thus suggesting that only an artifice can accurately establish a look, and that simply seeing what is there cannot; or he is deliberately switching to a symbolic plane, lending the camera trickery an inference which, far from momentarily identifying creator and character, separates them even further.

5. With the exception, of course, of Robert Montgomery's *The Lady in the Lake* (1947), where the camera adopts the viewpoint of the central character throughout.

31

2. The film-maker defines himself by his point of view towards the objects he reveals. This point of view is expressed first and foremost by the distance maintained by the camera. The distance between the camera and its objects varies, and this variation constitutes a sort of first gauge for cinematic reality (or irreality) and for any analysis. In Lang's work it manifests itself in a manner that may be open or veiled, so that the fascination and the difficulty one experiences in watching his films is constantly maintained throughout its many deviations.

From hundreds of examples I cite an almost theoretical one from *The Blue Gardenia*. Lang uses three shots to conjure his three heroines in bed in the apartment they share:

— The camera focuses in close-up on a pulp thriller, then retreats to reveal Rose sprawling in bed, bathed in light from the lamp she hasn't switched off.

— In a static shot, the camera focuses broadly on the sleeping Crystal, who mutters the name of her boy-friend.

— In long shot, the camera focuses on the corner of the room containing Norah's bed, and tracks forward until it is isolated; only then do we see Norah in closer shot (for she is the central character), listening to a radio under the bedclothes.

Distance, the impression of distance, depends equally importantly on the play of forms within the image. Hence, always in Lang, the intensification of perception through unexpected avenues. In the shadowy house of *Secret Beyond the Door*, the limpid, receding lines of an engraving in Miss Robey's office catch the eye, as though supplementing it. Similarly, when Kent and his girl Lilli sit discussing their bafflement in a café in *The Testament of Dr Mabuse*, there is a window in the upper half of the frame through which may be seen a long white avenue, seemingly unreal, whose vertiginous depths become even more pronounced when a passer-by appears, only his head visible, and crosses the screen. One might also cite a shot in *Siegfried*, bathed almost entirely in white; near a bench, against a light background of foliage, the young bridal pair are conversing gracefully, but above the trees, five wide arches emerging from the shadows seem to break up the image, the contrast leaving a sense of estrangement which disrupts the vision and offers a subterranean intimation as to the fatal outcome of the affair.

Also to be noted is the play on distance articulated, not on the relationship between fixed masses, but on movement within the frame. For example — almost a thematic element, so often is the narrative supported by them — doors opening and closing, constantly modifying space depending on whether they reveal more hidden depths or not, depending on the lighting, their placement; the doors one finds in every Lang film, particularly in the Chinese quarter of *Die Spinnen*, the cemetery in *Der müde Tod*, throughout *The Tiger of Eschnapur* and *The Indian Tomb*, but with a redoubled urgency when Harald Berger threads through the corridors, with the doors closing behind him, to emerge in the tiger-pit.

Similarly with the queen's cloaks in *Kriemhild's Revenge*, cloaks with vast folds that rise and fall, sometimes to an extent where they radically modify formal relationships within the shot. Kriemhild, for instance, addresses the horde of Huns from the top of a staircase; and her cloak, black and lustreless inside, glitteringly decorated on the outside, subjects the images to a strange interplay of shadows and surfaces depending upon whether the queen raises her arms or lets them fall to her side. A device which Lang was to recall in *Spione* and use again less theatrically, more in tune with the narrative thrust of the images, when the beautiful Sonia swirls her immense black and silver lamé cloak around Haighi in the same oppositional interplay.

3. There are innumerable formal or thematic pointers, devices which function from film to film and weave the enigmatic tracery of the Langian web. For instance the mark, the token around which the narrative is structured, the significant object which Lang always calls attention to with a close-up, a first, readily identifiable link from the visual to the thematic chain. To draw up an inventory of the maps, plans, letters, photographs, all the multifarious pointers which blaze a trail through Lang's forty films — from the seal affixed to the fateful document in *Der müde Tod* to the greasepaint mark on Berger's shirt in *The Indian Tomb* — would be a lengthy task. To do so would be to establish, through the script and underlying it, a definable series, of the sort one might call an 'acteme series', materialised in the images by one or more formal series: the close-up invariable in these circumstances, for example, is very often followed in the sound films, especially the American ones, by a dolly back from the object abruptly introduced. This short, precise movement, placing the object in its context, disrupts the close-up's sudden fascination, circumscribing it.

I shall cite only three examples, all from the same film, *Scarlet Street*. Opening a sequence, a flower in close-up; the movement reveals Christopher lovingly painting the flower given to him by Kitty. Later a letter lying among other things on a table; the movement which reveals Kitty's flat for the first time is also a precise indication of the relationship between Christopher and the young woman, since it is, as we immediately discover, a letter from him. And the dolly shot provoked in Kitty's new flat by Johnny's hat, hidden with ironic emphasis in close-up, needs no dialogue to aid its definition of the respective position of the three characters in this stringently cruel remake of Renoir's *La Chienne*.

4. The general, more or less intensified partialisation of space, which precipitates the eye into its most appropriate position, carries a dialectic of subject and object, originating in the German cultural tradition and

culminating in the basic materiality of the industrial civilisation, to its extreme limits in screen space: the object, as soon as it takes on a particular importance within the development of the action, seems to acquire through the intensity of the images something of the same symbolic life as the bewitched objects in Hoffmann or Arnim; the subject, an errant body, is often no more than an object among others. There is a particularly striking inversion of this principle in the take-off sequence from *Frau im Mond*, between the rocket, which appears to be the only actor, and the characters, its props; and in *Human Desire*, between Jeff Warren and the locomotive when he drives it from the track to the sheds.

Disjunctive, provoking the eye, this subject/object interplay which creates an incredible gaping fissure in Lang's films, finds equilibrium in a particularly frequent and significant type of shot which redoubles the continuous/discontinuous dialectic characteristic of the Langian vision: the body of the subject and the body of the object, fragmented, united as two mechanisms in a single image, offer a perfect example of the partialisation of space. In *Man Hunt*, for instance, the huge close-up of the hero's hand repeatedly hesitating over the trigger of his rifle. And in *Spione*, two forearms, the heavy, round handle of a safe which the hands are trying to turn; the dull gleam of the black leather raincoat corresponds to the lighter gleam of steel, and both to the whiteness of the hands: right from the outset, this being the opening shot, Lang places his film under the sign of the enigmatic division of space.

5. Like any film-maker, but more systematically and more insidiously than the rest, Lang bases the potential of his narrative on the richness and perversity of oppositions in the series of identical configurations.

These can be traced from film to film, a perpetual interplay between the same questions and different answers; to describe them in all their precision, identifying the kinds of opposition simultaneously set up in the images, sound, performances and narrative, would in itself provide the material for a unique inventory whose scope, and indeed significance, is difficult to define. But this interplay depends on the substructure of *mise en scène* and vision. Here are two examples, for simplicity's sake taken once again from the same film, *While the City Sleeps*.

— Walter Kyne Jr. and Edward Mobley are talking in the editor's office. A static long shot: visible from left to right: Kyne Jr., standing, dressed in black; higher up, against the wall, the portrait of Walter Kyne, his father, also wearing black; then, through the window, the city, its grey mass, spiky and regular; and finally Mobley, seated, dressed in grey. The four principal elements in the shot are all at different distances from the camera; the tones are divided two by two. A few moments later, following some brief detail shots of the different protagonists, Lang returns to the same long shot from a barely different angle. But the elements have changed; from left to right: Kyne Jr., Mobley, the painting, the city. The distances have altered. Mobley gets up, the camera follows his movement. In two shots identical in form a triple opposition comes into play, through the redistribution of actors, tonalities, distance, with each supporting the other two, initiating the last (stasis/movement), through which the narrative's progression is manifested.

— The bar in which journalists on the *New York Sentinel* meet. Again a static long shot. We see Mobley sitting at the counter, and the barman standing; at the back of the room, a staircase we can barely see rises to the left. We wait; Lang prolongs the edgy silence of the image. Until finally, arriving with the intention of making advances to Mobley, Mildred appears on the staircase. Why the wait in such a simple shot? Because a few sequences earlier Lang had filmed precisely the same space and we had been made to wait then, almost light-heartedly, but no one came down the stairs.

6. Lang thus keeps the eye in perpetual hesitation; because the event, either foreseen or already past, always seems linked to something else, something palpable in its authority, which one has no way of defining, but which is incapable of imposing itself in its own right. This waiting, dissymmetrical in nature, through which the film cunningly plays on a constant imbalance, is used flagrantly — and so with deliberate abstraction — in a shot, a configuration deriving from both narrative and vision, which reappears throughout Lang's work. The principle is simple. It consists of a static long shot in three parts, two actions separated by a moment of stasis. A character goes out of frame, the camera remains fixed on the setting, another character enters the frame by another way (or it may be, though it rarely is, the same character returning the same way). The setting at such moments always has a particular beauty, pregnant with meaning and possibilities: the police inspector's office in the first *Mabuse*, the corridor outside the doctor's office in the second, the staircase and landing leading to the apartments of the two young women in *While the City Sleeps*, the subterranean passageways under the palace in *The Tiger of Eschnapur* and *The Indian Tomb*. The characters are linked by the event that is poised to happen; this shot almost invariably occurs at moments of great dramatic intensity. Adopting this method of disrupting the standard development of a plot, Lang impairs the narrative and, seemingly at least, distorts time in favour of pure scrutiny, thereby conferring a sense of strangeness on the action that is thus stretched out, and on the suddenly ominous, insistent vision; the result is more or less what Lang achieves for vision alone, in a much briefer and more compact shot, when he assembles his elements in such a way that the eye always seems to be in the wrong place, either too close or too far away. In *Siegfried*, for instance: three

warriors occupy almost the entire surface of the screen; they are so close that they cannot be seen in their entirety; between them are blank spaces, in the background a bare wall; the image is perfectly flat and the soldiers look like cardboard cutouts; when Kriemhild's women pass behind them, following her, perspective suddenly returns so vividly that one feels it as being too deep, and it seems like another illusion.

7. Because Lang plays a highly perverse game. It is through the lacunae, the lack he establishes, that he seems intelligible. And it is this which requires decipherment at all levels. More than any other film-maker, Lang works counter to his images. Starting here, examination reveals that at the film's other extreme, as it were, Lang this time plays the counter game against the script. Since he throws his images off balance by extending them, he throws his narrative off course, lets a veil descend over his characters. Therefore, as Luc Moullet has noted, he works against genre, even in America, adopting but insidiously undermining the traditional rules. He incorporates both the principle and its destruction. What are *Frau im Mond, Rancho Notorious, Moonfleet, Beyond a Reasonable Doubt, The Tiger of Eschnapur* and *The Indian Tomb* in relation to science fiction, the Western, the adventure film, the thriller and exotic romance but ventures in rank subversion?

There remains the question of why Lang is so concerned with disjunction. To leave repeatedly in his work the signs of a pervasive defeat, revealed by the hopelessness of a dead-end, entirely self-enclosed system. Crevices seem to appear in the dense texture of Lang's films, as if he were always anxious to make the precariousness of the real world clearly visible, and to show how illusory is the notion of a harmony achieved through a total autonomy in its representation. Between one shot and the next, and from one end of the film to the other, a clearly defined, divisive *mise en scène* takes shape, always concerned in any of its constituent effects to maintain the impulse behind the whole, to impress the body of its material with the creative imagination's constant reflection on itself; and to do so with even greater stringency when the cinema gains new expressive possibilities along with technical mastery, and the camera becomes possessed of the magic which makes it so difficult for us to follow it: becoming, as it brushes against the life it espouses while attempting to pin it down, 'an actor of great importance, mobile, *living*'. So with Lang, in a sense, the film always seems to be constructing itself as it goes along. We sense the effort, the temptation offered by possibilities, the distance between the wish and its object, something akin to a typical manifestation of a *mise en scène* assured of its power, but invariably a little dishevelled and wearied too. Hence the fascination and the sense of remoteness always aroused by his superb films. And the feeling that, with him, *mise en scène,* and *mise en scène* alone, attains to myth.

(Translated by Tom Milne)

STEPHEN JENKINS

Lang: Fear and Desire

It is arguable that the most significant developments in film theory during the last ten years or so, certainly in the area of classical narrative cinema, have occurred around ideas involving the representation of women. This phrase covers a variety of approaches which have produced important advances in the study of, for example, stereotyping, genre, psychoanalysis and cinema, and so on. As a result it would now be unjustifiable to produce a book of this kind which was not inflected by these general developments in film theory.

The aim here is to account for the stylistic aspects of the Lang-text generally, and to describe a part of it in some detail, in terms other than those which have previously dominated writing on Lang. This previous approach can be summed up in a sentence: 'The Lang-text represents various manifestations of the person Lang's fatalistic world view.' This idea of fate in Lang can perhaps be most usefully displaced by constructing a reading which inserts — forcefully — the question of the significance of the female presence within the Lang-text. It remains to emphasise that the films described here were not specially selected, but were those films which were accessible for viewing at the time of writing.

A curious pattern of paranoia runs through Lang's films from the first *Mabuse* in 1922 to the last in 1961 . . . Lang makes sentimental exceptions to this paranoia in the pure, trustworthy love of beautiful girls, a love capable of destroying the most intricately insidious conspiracies ever devised by evil minds.

Andrew Sarris, *The American Cinema*

Women play a prominent role in Lang's world, but for the most part they embody the destructive forces of the environment into which the hero is thrust . . . Lang has made a great many 'femme fatale' films . . . The conception of character is archetypal; these women personify destructive and violent erotic drives, but they are never explored in any depth.

Claire Johnston, notes for BFI Study Unit 10, *Fritz Lang*

Lang . . . sometimes allows his characters to soften and the tension of their wills to slacken; but for him this is also the moment to relax the tension of his thought, to let it seek respite from the concept with the object it caresses and which nourishes it. So scenes of contemplation and repose abound, usually favouring the female characters . . . There is, however, nothing sensual about these moments of pure abeyance which one so distinctly feels to be turned towards some *elsewhere*.

Philippe Demonsablon, *The Imperious Dialectic of Fritz Lang*

Raymond Bellour, in the article reprinted in this volume, writes of a certain ambiguity, a hesitancy, in the 'systems of vision' within Lang's *mise en scène*, which he construes as 'a distance between desire and its object'. As the quotations above suggest an ambiguity, to the point of contradiction, around the function of women in Lang's work, it would seem useful to bring these areas together, to examine the place of women within the system of representations/narratives which bear Lang's name, of which he is 'the man-subject behind the camera' (Bellour's phrase again), the generator of the worshipped *mise en scène*. This may be useful in attempting to move criticism of the Lang-text beyond the blockage formed around it by the idea of Fate, which always renders the text as closed in on itself, endlessly repeating 'the same bleak view of the universe where man grapples with his personal destiny, and inevitably loses' (Andrew Sarris), where the functions of 'man' and 'woman' (and what those terms signify) must be fixed for the fatal pattern to emerge. If one wishes to 'unfix', to problematise, the Lang-text then one needs to open up the terms of the man/woman/destiny triangle, and perhaps develop the implications of another remark by Sarris, that 'there is something of the voyeur in Lang'.

The terms of a relationship between notions of 'style', the representation of women, and the look/desire axis have been suggested by Paul Willemen in 'The Ophuls Text: A Thesis' (in *Ophuls*, edited by Paul Willemen, British Film Institute 1978). He describes Ophuls' cinema as 'the dramatisation of repression, where the repressed returns and imprints its mark on the representation, undermining, and at times overwhelming that manifestation of secondary elaboration called "a coherent scenario".' According to Willemen, in Ophuls' work 'the camera is on the side of the Law, but it is the repressed which moves it along, obsessively circling its object of fascination . . . The cinema . . . comes to stand under the sign of the look at that which is socially withheld, reactivating as an institution specifically designed for this, the nexus look/desire and scene/seen. According to the rules of patriarchy, it is at this intersection that the figure of woman is produced as image . . . the signifier of desire'.

The look at the female becomes the point on which turns a dialectic of order and excess. Willemen describes three levels in the films which are marked by this dialectic. First, the narrative is fragmented and distorted by the 'impact of the scopic drive . . . The linear, orderly telling of the story from beginning to end breaks open, turns back on itself . . . the perpetual recommencing of the story, the renewal of the trajectory, the repetition or doubling of scenes'. Secondly, the arrangement of the pro-filmic event combines/opposes ` symmetry/balance in terms of characters and other characters, characters and objects, characters and mirrors, doubled elements in the sets, shapes in the sets etc., and, on the other hand, 'a proliferation of excessive detail, filling up the image with impediments to the look, obstacles between scene and seen, as well as the proliferation of objects in the sets themselves'. Thus 'the look is simultaneously subjected to two forces, pulling it in different directions'. Thirdly, 'there is the conduct of the camera, the combination of restlessness, ceaseless movement . . . with repetitions of movements at different times, although often accompanying a doubled scene on the level of the narrative . . . The tracks, dollys and crane movements constantly holding out the promise that in passing or in the shift from one look to another . . . the look may find its object of desire'.

I would now like to apply the terms of Willemen's account of Ophuls' work to the Lang-text.

1. *Women*

Willemen notes that Ophuls' films tend to 'focus on women . . . women tend to be produced as pivots within intricate and elaborate narrative structures, and as privileged objects of the look, that of the audience as well as that of intra-diegetic characters'. Within the Lang-text, only *Destiny, Kriemhild's Revenge* and *Clash by Night* can be said to centre on female protagonists. Other films, such as *Secret Beyond the Door* and *The Blue Gardenia*, investigate the possibility of such a centring, but ultimately privilege male discourses of which the female is firmly marked as object (rather than 'pivot'). But with Lang the woman is rarely unproblematic as object. What tends to happen is that the very idea of the female is dealt with by various forms of displacement. Woman becomes a memory from outside the space of the text which haunts the male central character. Thus Kai Hoog in Part 2 of *Die Spinnen* flashes back to the murder of the Inca priestess at the end of Part 1. Similarly, Stephen Neale in *The Ministry of Fear* is haunted by the memory of his dead wife, whom he poisoned in a 'mercy killing'. A crucial factor in the central relationship between Jeremy Fox and the boy John Mohune in *Moonfleet* is the memory of the absent first point in the mother/father/son triangle. The motor for the narrative of *Beyond a Reasonable Doubt* is the unsolved murder of Patti Grey. The violent death of a female character *within* the text's present tense — for instance the rape and murder of

Vern Haskell's fiancé in *Rancho Notorious*, or the murder of Dave Bannion's wife in the *The Big Heat* — is often a trigger which drives the narrative on, through the compulsive desire for revenge which then affects the male character.

Alternatively, this desire for revenge can produce the impression of circularity, of the narrative recommencing rather than terminating, as in the case of *Man Hunt*, which ends with Thorndike, having learned of the murder of Jenny by Nazi agents, parachuting into Germany with the intention of 'stalking' Hitler again, as in the film's opening sequence. In cases like these, woman, always associated with death, is an essential presence for the narrative process, but only in the form of an absence. A marked example of this would be the 'empty place' at table set for Elsie Beckmann, one of the murder victims in *M*. The murdered woman is often replaced by a female character made strange in some way. Thus Debby Marsh in *The Big Heat* becomes woman as 'bearer of the wound', half her face covered to hide the flesh disfigured by scalding coffee. Altar Kean in *Rancho Notorious* first appears in the film's 'present' dressed in male clothing, as opposed to her depiction in the flashbacks as the quintessential saloon girl, a 'glory girl' as she is remembered by Dolly. And both these films end with the female presence once more violently repressed (both women shot dead), the narratives closing on images of unstable all-male equilibrium: Bannion is reinstated with the police force, Vern Haskell and Frenchy Fairmont ride away together. Woman often signifies the literal return of the repressed, where the latter is the memory of murder. Thus Marjorie Byrne appears at the top of the stairs in *House by the River*, momentarily becoming the 'ghost' of Emily Gaunt, the maid murdered by Stephen Byrne. Dolly Moore, in *Beyond a Reasonable Doubt*, takes the place of the dead Patti Gray, as the latter's murder is re-enacted.

A second form of displacement involving woman as object is a number of substitutions for, or doublings of, the female image in the Lang-text. In its most extreme form this becomes pure fetishism, as in *Metropolis* where a piece of cloth found by Freder signifies Maria, or in *Spione* where Sonja is replaced by the madonna and child medallion which she gives to Tremaine, or *Man Hunt* where the arrow pin signifies Jenny, or *Rancho Notorious* where Haskell's fiancée becomes a memory signified by the brooch for which he searches. Often the relation between the sign for the woman and the actual female character represented within the text is more directly iconic. Thus Maria in *Metropolis* is doubled by the figure of the robot. The reflected image of Alice Reed in *Woman in the Window* appears within the same (picture) frame as its painted double. Kitty Marsh in *Scarlet Street* is doubled by the portrait painted by Chris Cross. The sanctity of gangster Mike Lagana's home in *The Big Heat* is represented by the painting of his mother which hangs in his study. In the same film Debby Marsh and Bertha Duncan reflect each other's

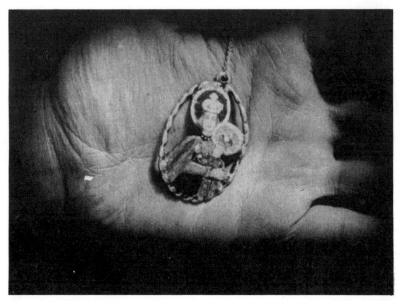

Woman reduced to fetish (*Spione*)

The female image doubled: Maria and robot (*Metropolis*)

The female image doubled: Alice Reed and her portrait (*Woman in the Window*)

Kitty Marsh's portrait (*Scarlet Street*)

The direct gaze as excess (*While the City Sleeps*)

image ('sisters under the mink').

The significance of these various displacements, substitutes and doublings is perhaps suggested by their opposite. In the pre-credits sequence of *While the City Sleeps*, for instance, the gaze of the camera/spectator at the woman is heavily marked as 'direct' — she screams into, and gazes back at, the camera as it tracks towards her. What is signified by this moment of excess is both desire and her death, for the third 'look' involved is that of the 'Lipstick Killer', a sex murderer, with whose point of view the camera gaze is also at this moment identified. The core of the narrative, the after-credits sequence, concerns efforts to contain this excess, to catch the killer. In terms of the investigation shown the look at the body of the woman is repressed, a point explicitly made by the pan from a shot of a bath robe, signifying/replacing the murdered woman's body, to the police photographer who is photographing the garment. A later victim is signified by an outline of her body drawn in chalk. The spectator sees the victim's face only as part of a close-up of a newspaper front page, where the image of the face is framed as an insert within an image entitled 'Scene of Latest Slaying' — image within image within image, frame within frame within frame. If one flashes back to *Scarlet Street*, this image is mirrored — a newspaper front page in close-up bearing the headline 'Ice Pick Murder In Greenwich Village', with the victim's image beneath.

44

While the City Sleeps

Scarlet Street

45

2. Narrative Structure

Individual narrative structures within the Lang-text are noticeably unconvoluted, unfragmented, undistorted. Just as the look at the woman, in contrast to Ophuls, is affected by displacement in the ways outlined above, so 'the past' is often present in the text only as that which is repressed from the text's present tense. Woman as memory has already been mentioned. One might also cite Kent's memory of the murder of his sweetheart and best friend in *Testament of Dr Mabuse*; the similar idea of the criminal past haunting the present in *You Only Live Once* and *You and Me*; the familial relationship from the past which must be repressed for the sake of a character's stability in the present, as with the knowledge that Vance Shaw and Jack Slade in *Western Union* are brothers; or the previously mentioned relationships in *Moonfleet*. In *Clash by Night* it is the notion of Mae Doyle's past life in general which is incompatible with the image of woman as loyal wife and mother demanded of her by Jerry in the film's present.

The past rarely emerges in the present as an unproblematic flashback which simply serves to convey information necessary for the comprehension or clarification of the narrative's present. Two examples where this does occur are *Die Spinnen* Part 2, as Kai Hoog flashes back to the death of the Inca priestess at the end of Part 1 (a necessary structural feature of the serial), and *Testament of Dr Mabuse*, when a flashback reveals the basis of Tom's relationship with Lilli. Subsequently in the Lang-text flashbacks have a resonance which goes beyond the function of merely providing necessary additional illustrations for the present. But they do not express the disturbance caused when the repressed ruffles the textual fabric, as with Ophuls.

In *Liliom* and *Fury* the flashbacks are specifically marked as *replays* of images from the film's own past, reseen in its present, and with the source of the replayed images distinguished from the (sourceless) meta-discourse of the film as a whole — the newsreel film in *Fury* showing the burning of the jail, and the celestial television in *Liliom* replaying moments from the central character's life. In a sense these are denials of the normal function of flashbacks, i.e. the clarification of the present. Rather they specifically question the status of filmic images as unproblematic, objective representations of truth; they call into question what the spectator has previously been shown. In both *You and Me* and *The Return of Frank James* the past is not flashed back to. Instead what is shown is the process of re-creating a version of the past. Both versions are marked as fantasy. The ex-convicts' memory of their woman-free prison life in *You and Me* is characterised by extreme visual and aural disturbance which, like the opening song/montage and the lecture delivered by Helen, breaks up the (comparatively) naturalistic flow of the narrative. In *The Return of Frank James*, Jesse James' murder is re-enacted by the Fords as a stage performance, a deliberately falsified

dramatic fantasy of the past within the fantasy of the film's present.
Woman in the Window and *Scarlet Street*, the two films by Lang most
usefully considered within the context of *film noir*, are noticeably free of
the flashbacks which are a major structural component of many films
within that category. The revelation that most of the narrative of *Woman
in the Window* has the status of a dream clearly has resonance with regard
to the status/meaning of depicted events, but does not affect the
'readability' of the narrative's progression. The labyrinthine structure
characteristic of *film noir* is often linked with an attempt to circumscribe
the mystery associated with the *femme fatale*. In these two Lang films this
fantasy is displaced by the very idea of the representation of the female
body as object of the male gaze. In *Woman in the Window* the portrait of the
woman 'comes to life' as Professor Wanley gazes at it. In *Scarlet Street*
Chris Cross attempts to fix Kitty's image by painting her portrait. One
might compare, for example, John Brahm's *The Locket* (1946), where the
male investigation of the female central character, in terms of her
character, produces a series of flashback within flashback within flashback. The starting point for this complex structure is the desire of one
man to inform another of the 'truth' concerning the woman the latter is
about to marry. With Lang there is no such investigation of psychological 'truth', but instead representation, image within image. Women are
significantly doubled by their painted images in other examples of 40s
film noir/melodrama, including *Laura* (1944), *Rebecca* (1940) and indeed
The Locket, but, unlike the Lang films, these images function as
metaphors for the surface, the mystery which must be penetrated for a
truth to be revealed. In *Woman in the Window* and *Scarlet Street* there is only
surface; it is the significance of representation itself which is directly
investigated.

The flashback and the enigma of the female *are* linked in *Rancho
Notorious*, but whereas with Ophuls it is the look at the woman which
causes the narrative ceaselessly to 'turn back on itself [as a result of] the
impact of the scopic drive' (Willemen), with the Lang film quite the
opposite occurs. The scopic drive becomes the subject of the narrative's
present, that with which it deals, by a form of play around the idea of the
look. Vern Haskell is looking, i.e. searching, for the murderers of his
fiancée. It is this look(ing) which drives the narrative forward, a drive
expressed in the song which comments on his actions: 'the old, old story
of Hate, Murder and Revenge'. But this search is heavily marked by a
look, a gaze, on Haskell's part. When he first learns of the Chuck A Luck
ranch from a dying outlaw, the question asked by the song, 'Where or
what is Chuck A Luck', is juxtaposed with a close-up of Haskell gazing at
the camera/spectator. Finding the killers becomes very much a question
of the look finding its object. 'He looks straight through a man,'
comments one of the outlaws at the ranch. 'You're always using your
eyes,' says Altar Kean. Because he cannot verbalise his quest (he is in the

Searching as looking (*Rancho Notorious*)

ranch under false pretences) Haskell can only stare — not only at the men he suspects, but also at his fiancée's brooch, the fetish object now worn by Altar, and at Altar herself. What he can verbalise is his (feigned?) desire for Altar. This, he tells her, after we have watched him watching her playing the piano, framed by the window he stands outside, is the reason he 'keeps coming back' to the ranch. He claims that he 'likes a woman like a pipe dream'. This link between the male gaze and its female object posited as somehow imaginary is a reference back to the first occasion when Haskell sees Altar. He stares at her. 'What did you think I was . . . a pipe dream?' she asks. Haskell's realisation that Kinch is the object of his search, the murderer, the man he is looking for, coincides with his attempt to make Altar imagine the dead body of his fiancée on the floor in front of her, i.e. the woman as imaginary, the impossible object his look can no longer find.

The significance of the flashbacks in the first half of the film to Altar Kean's early days is that they permit the depiction of the woman as unproblematic object of desire, in contrast to the film's present, through the stereotype of the 'fiery', 'wilful' saloon girl. This stereotype is balanced at the beginning of the film by an alternative: woman as object of desire, but also as lynchpin of the social order. The film opens with a close-up of Haskell and his fiancée embracing. The connotations of the kiss are quickly established — marriage (they are to be married in eight days), the home (she will call the ranch 'The Last Cloud') and children (they intend to have a large family). The 'wider' implications are underlined by the fact that the town is deserted because everyone has gone to see the Burton triplets. Once this image of woman has been violently obliterated through rape and murder, then it returns only in a distorted form. Within the alternative society of Chuck A Luck Altar switches between female and male roles, functions and dress; the object of desire is problematised. Haskell's quest can be read as having a repressed homosexual aim which will be fulfilled at the film's conclusion. Altar steps in front of a bullet intended for Frenchy Fairmont. This sacrifice enables the Haskell/Frenchy/Altar triangle of emotions to be resolved with Haskell united with Frenchy, the presence of the female having been dealt with as violently as it was with Beth, the murdered fiancée.

The trajectory of the narrative in terms of the female presence can thus be summarised as follows:

a) Presence (Beth) which is then violently repressed.
b) Presence, but only in the memory/fantasy of Altar's past, which as much signifies absence, that which is lost.
c) Presence, but only in an ambiguous form, i.e. Altar's female/male role-switching.
d) Presence, but only as the memory of the absent Beth, which Haskell tries to force Altar to confront.
e) Presence, but only as that which must be, once again, violently repressed/sacrificed (the death of Altar), in order for the film to conclude with
f) Absence, heavily marked, as Haskell and Frenchy Fairmont ride away together.

Exactly what is repressed from the narrative is the 'unproblematic' female presence, a repression underlined by the status of the flashbacks, where such a presence is possible, and which are inserts that break up the straightforward temporal drive from a) to f), but without threatening the control inherent in this drive.

In both *Secret Beyond the Door* and *The Blue Gardenia*, flashbacks occur which illustrate a specifically female discourse within the surrounding meta-discourse of the narrative; but again, these serve only to reaffirm the control inherent in the narrative movement, rather than, as with Ophuls, radically to undermine that control. Celia's memories at the beginning of *Secret Beyond the Door* establish her as troubled by something she cannot understand, an enigma solvable only when she is constituted as the object of Mark's discourse, becomes the 'you' opposed to his 'I'. As he puts it, 'You're not what you think you are'. In *The Blue Gardenia*, Rose flashes back to the murder of Prebble, the depiction of her guilt enabling the crucial gap in Norah's memory to be filled. This is a result of Casey Mayo's intervention, since it is he who picks up on the musical clue which solves the problem. In the first case the flashback is associated with the female as enigma, in the second with the female as dangerous, but in both cases the flashback serves to bracket, close off, the trouble. The break in the narrative's temporal flow signifies the containment of excess, rather than being in itself the signifier of that excess.

The latter tendency culminates in *Beyond a Reasonable Doubt*. The narrative content of the film's present (the 'framing' of Tom Garrett) is a (re)presentation within that present of a past process leading to a moment of excess (the murder of Patti Grey), the 'actual' depiction of which is of necessity repressed in order that the question of Garrett's innocence or guilt can be posited at all. Up to the moment of Garrett's arrest the film can be read as depicting the construction of a flashback, a demonstration of the previously mentioned notion of control, of closing off, but simultaneously a disavowal of any implication that such control guarantees or implies 'truth'. What is being undermined is exactly the status of what constitutes 'proof' or 'evidence'.

3. *Symmetry/Excess*

The status of the relationships between characters, sets, decor and objects within the *mise en scène* of the Lang-text has long been a mainstay of critical writing on it. There are two main extra-textual reasons for this interest.

The first is the association of Lang's early German work with the ill-defined notion of 'German Expressionist cinema'. The bracketing of the German cinema of the immediate post-World War One period has signified, according to the crudest definitions, two things. First, the notion of art as opposed to commerce: 'By no means all films are produced from the commercial factory only interested in profit. After the first World War the German government subsidised the German film industry and founded a national school of cinema which was an important element in the development of the art. It is represented by the early work of Fritz Lang' (Roger Manvell, *Film,* revised edition 1946). Secondly, that the identifiable stylistic and thematic characteristics of this cinema were the result and expression of a nationalistic world view: 'German cinema had its most influential period in the years following World War I when depression and despair drove directors into a macabre fantasy world . . . Fritz Lang seemed primarily interested in the criminal mentality though he produced master-works of prophecy and Teutonic legend' (Leslie Halliwell, *The Filmgoer's Companion,* 3rd edition 1970). The essence of the art had to do with the status of the pro-filmic event, as opposed, essentially, to ideas around montage. The simple equation was between the artificial, anti-naturalistic pro-filmic world and the 'real world' inhabited by the audience, to which the former was linked by virtue of 'mood'. Thus: 'Its undeniable atmospheric power was due to acting, setting and lighting. The German technicians, with great feeling for their macabre and sombre subjects in the depression after the

50

war, produced a series of masterpieces for showing to their equally depressed audiences who visited the unheated cinemas in a mood of fatalism' (Manvell, op. cit.).

The twin strands of this argument have been refined and developed through various writings. Lotte Eisner, in *The Haunted Screen,* has discussed the various cultural inputs, as opposed to vague notions of Expressionism, which shaped the pro-filmic world of the films; and the relationship between the films and their social base has been examined by, for example, Siegfried Kracauer in *From Caligari to Hitler,* and Andrew Tudor in *Image and Influence.* But if the critical discourses have become more sophisticated, the basic significance of the decor, sets and lighting (the constituent elements of the pro-filmic world) has been read in similar terms to Manvell's. Thus Tudor writes:

Whether distortion depends primarily on the grotesque angles and impossible perspectives of expressionist design, or the strange shadings of the chiaroscuro tradition, seems immaterial. Generally there is a mixture and the result is largely the same. A world at odds with itself, peopled by the phantoms of both mind and spirit . . . disharmony is the keynote, whatever the melody. The tortured characters of the German silent cinema are part of an alien malevolent world, permeated by fate. They are constrained by the unknown; powerful forces wash over them; their world is dislocated within itself. They must inevitably pay Faust's price. Of course this cluster of meanings is very generalised. By its nature artistic style deals in such generalities. It communicates an ethos, a mood, a sense of fatalism and disorder. The whole pictorial character of these visuals makes a mockery of harmony between man and environment (*Image and Influence,* p. 160).

The fact that the decor, lighting, etc., command as much attention as the characters becomes crucial for establishing the notion of fate as a key term in discussion of the German section of the Lang-text. Julian Petley's description of *Destiny* exemplifies this view: 'Lang's obsession with Fate is expressed visually as much as by plot: the characters are frequently dwarfed and overshadowed by the huge sets, imprisoned by and reduced to geometrical elements of the decor. Thus Lang's *mise en scène* renders perfectly the feeling of domination which the Fate-governed universe evokes in man, a feeling heightened by Lang's lighting: shadows loom large around the characters and highlight the threatening and imprisoning forms of their surroundings' (*BFI Distribution Library Catalogue,* 1978).

The second extra-textual reason for this interest is basically biographical and consists of an assumed association between the person Lang and the subject of architecture. The fact that Lang briefly studied architecture can initially be tied in with ideas about German silent films

51

and film-makers in general. Thus: 'Many of the German silent directors had in fact a visual rather than a literary background. Lang trained as an architect, Murnau was an art historian, Leni a painter. The soul of the films is always in the surface offered to the eye. *Metropolis* is a metronome and protractor film' (Raymond Durgnat, *Films and Feelings*, 1967). The architect factor becomes important as regards Lang in particular in the auteurist attempt to seal the gap between the German and American periods. If Lang's work is 'based on a metaphysic of architecture', as ·Claude Chabrol claims, then this is because 'As a stylist Lang has remained faithful to the principles of the silent films of the early twenties. He creates his effects within static frameworks, by composition and exact editing' (Nicholas Garnham, 'The Dark Struggle' in *Film* (GB), no. 32). The architect factor emerges occasionally in the American and later German films as an element of narrative content (Mark Lamphere in *Secret Beyond the Door* edits a journal of architecture, Harald Berger in *The Tiger of Eschnapur* is an architect), but in critical writing on Lang it becomes merged with ideas concerning his treatment of characters, objects, space, etc. Thus 'Lang has certain personal idiosyncrasies. He likes to frame characters against blank walls to highlight their actions, and consistently uses sets and props to make points — for example the towering geometry of the forests in *Siegfried,* the shopfronts in *The Woman in the Window* and *You and Me,* the articles on the dressing table in *House by the River*' (Garnham, op. cit.). What was seen as a feature of German silent cinema as a whole becomes a mark of Lang's consistency: 'His themes and preoccupations, revolving around the various manifesta-tions of Fate, remain constant, and his style . . . evolves consistently and coherently towards ever greater abstraction and simplicity . . . His handling of space, and in particular his geometric placing of actors, establishing a sense of pre-ordained ritual and integrating them with the decor so that they seem about as free as statues on a building, remains remarkably constant' (Petley, op. cit.).

The problem with this view of the Lang-text is that it can veer dangerously towards a kind of formalism. It is interesting that Julian Petley quotes Luc Moullet, on *Secret Beyond the Door,* as follows: 'Lang plays solely on the hallucinatory fascination of the subject, on the mysteriousness of the action, on the ultra-modern brilliance and beauty of the abstract decor. It is a film of pure *mise en scène,* a Marienbadian film of mirrors, keys, corridors, lamps and doors, all set within the framework of a strange country mansion.' However, Moullet goes on to say, though this is not quoted by Petley: 'This work is considered by the group of extremist aesthetes among the young French critics as a perfect masterpiece, a diamond of *mise en scène*; this admiration defines the film's limitations' (Luc Moullet, *Fritz Lang*). In other words, what does one say beyond an almost fetishistic description of the film's surface? The answer has generally been: talk about Fate. Characters are not simply trapped within patterns of precise design, their position is an emblematic expression of Lang's fatalistic world-view. Thus the gap between the visual pleasure afforded by individual images, and their significance within a *narrative* context, is bridged.

Similar terms have dominated discussion of Lang's use of objects. In complete contrast, once again, to Ophuls, objects in the Lang-text do not function as 'excessive detail', 'impediments to the look', 'obstacles between scene and seen', but emphatically as that which is the intended object of the spectator's gaze. As Raymond Bellour notes: 'There are innumerable formal or thematic pointers, devices which function from film to film and weave the enigmatic tracery of the Langian web. For instance the mark, the token around which the narrative is structured, the significant object which Lang always calls attention to with a close-up, a first, readily identifiable link from the visual to the thematic chain.' Obvious examples of objects which constitute such links include the madonna and child medallion in *Spione*, Eddie Taylor's initialled hat in *You Only Live Once*, the arrow pin in *Man Hunt*, the cake in *Ministry of Fear*, the initialled pencil in *The Woman in the Window*, flowers in *Scarlet Street* and *Secret Beyond the Door*, the brooch in *Rancho Notorious*. In terms of meaning (the thematic chain) these objects, like the relationship between characters and decor, are generally seen as pointed illustrations or expressions of Lang's fatalism. For example, Julian Petley writes of *Siegfried's Tod*: 'Siegfried's Fate, and thus the Fate of all the participants, is sealed right from the start when he is bathing in the dragon's blood which will make him immune to injury, and a leaf falls on him, leaving one part of his body vulnerable. Lang stresses this detail very carefully, and this leaf becomes the first of a series of objects in Lang's films which play a vital part in Fate's plan to bring about a character's downfall' (Petley, op. cit.).

But if one considers the fact that 'character' in discussion of Lang always actually means 'male character', and that, as previously suggested, the Lang-text is 'troubled' in various ways by the presence and depiction of the female, then it becomes significant that many of these objects can be read as having specific relevance outside vague notions of 'fate'. Rather they are examples of displacement of the female through substitution. Some objects are not directly interchangeable with a female character, but nevertheless function as emblems of a certain crucial disturbance within the narrative which is always traceable back to the idea of the female. Thus the cake which contains microfilm in *The Ministry of Fear* is symptomatic of the status of the world in which Stephen Neale finds himself when he is released from an asylum at the beginning of the film. This world reflects his feigned madness, which was his method of dealing with the fact that he killed his wife. The flowers worn by Celia in *Secret Beyond the Door* disturb Mark Lamphere because, it is ultimately revealed, they are associated with the moment when he

53

Thematic pointers: *You Only Live Once*

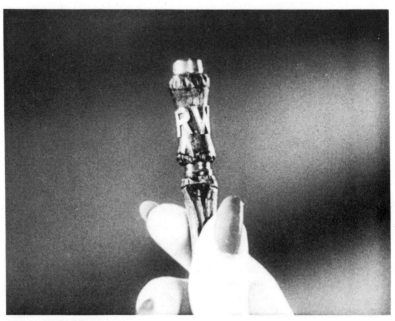

Woman in the Window

The Ministry of Fear

considers he was rejected by his mother. Richard Wanley's pencil in *The Woman in the Window* is seen in close-up, held in Alice Reed's fingers, signifying the impossibility of his escaping the consequences of his fantasy, whereby a woman in a painting was made flesh.

A link between the 'freezing' of characters as elements of decor and the concentration on significant objects is the further tendency within the Lang-text to isolate in close-up parts of the human body. Clearly this is not unique to Lang but it *is* a noticeable stylistic feature, and gains in significance when considered in conjunction with the aspects of style already mentioned. Examples abound: Masimoto's hand, upon which drops of rain are falling, as he sets off before his fatal encounter with Kitty in *Spione*; the hand marked with the letter M which will in turn mark Peter Lorre's shoulder in *M*; the shot of Hofmeister's foot at the beginning of *Testament of Dr Mabuse*; eyes peering through the rear window of the robbery car in *You Only Live Once*; Helen and Joe's hands meeting on the escalator rail in *You and Me*; a finger on the trigger in *Man Hunt*; the close-up of Chris Cross' crossed fingers in *Scarlet Street*, as he denies that he is superstitious. An image which recurs shows feet spread apart, with something fallen between them — drops of blood in *You Only Live Once*, from Eddie Taylor's slashed wrists; a kitchen knife in *Scarlet Street*; a comic-book in *While the City Sleeps*. One needs to distinguish between the specific narrative significance of such images, their narrative function, and their significance as symptoms of a textual tendency.

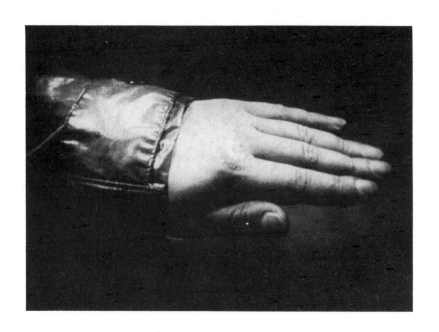

The body in close-up: (above) *Spione;* (below) *Testament of Dr Mabuse*

56

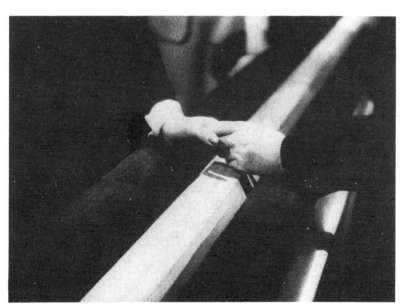

(above) *You Only Live Once*; (below) *You and Me*

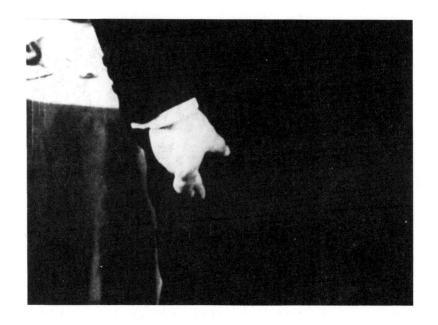

The body in close-up: (above) *Scarlet Street*; (below) *You Only Live Once*

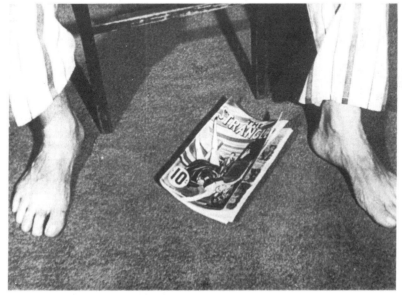

(above) *Scarlet Street*; (below) *While the City Sleeps* 59

These two areas have generally been collapsed together in critical discussion of the Lang-text. This is particularly apparent as regards the human face. Thus, if Lang has a 'penchant for rather expressionless actors like Dana Andrews' (Petley, op. cit.), then this is inevitably and automatically a further manifestation of the director's fatalism, whereby 'his characters have always been abstract and schematic, like pawns in a game, occupying a claustrophobically deterministic world'. But if one removes the idea of Fate then a different reading is possible. Expressionless faces, like the body dismembered by close-ups, like the body as an element of decor, like the substitution of objects for human figures, like the human figures who are crucial in their absence: all these factors can be read as textual symptoms of a certain disavowal of, a reticence over, mainstream narrative cinema's massive investment in the pleasurable gaze at the human figure. At one level, of course, this investment is obvious; but recent developments in the areas of psychoanalysis and cinema and the representation of women have greatly problematised this previously 'innocent' and taken for granted mechanism. Lang attempted to deny this disavowal: 'The film has made us witnesses of the magic of the human face, it has taught us to read what lies behind the silence of this face and has shown us the reaches of the human soul' (Lang, quoted by Georges Sadoul in *Dictionary of Film Makers*, translated by Peter Morris, University of California Press 1972). But his own work constantly denies this passage to 'truth' via the look at the human face. The most powerful instance of this denial occurs during *You Only Live Once*. Sylvia Sidney and Henry Fonda are placed face to face in the prison where she has come to visit him. For once the faces *are* isolated, each offered as stressed object of the gaze of the other (and of the spectator), albeit framed within the frame and behind glass. Yet what the scene is about, the narrative point, is exactly a difficulty of communication. If Fonda's face bears what Truffaut described as a 'look of chilling intensity', then the meaning of this intensity is firmly displaced on to the soundtrack — he is telling her to get him a gun, forced to whisper so that, as Truffaut points out, 'we only hear the consonants — just the guttural sounds of the two g's and the t'.

4. *Camera movement*

The difference between the Ophuls and Lang texts is most marked stylistically at the level of camera movement. Andrew Sarris wrote that Ophuls gave 'camera movement its finest hours in the history of the cinema'. With Lang, camera movements are both rare and highly functional. This is not to suggest a lapse into formalism with regard to the Ophuls text. Both Sarris and Willemen, for example, attempt to locate Ophuls' camera movements within (very different) frames of meaning. But critical writing on the Lang-text has constantly stressed *composition* as the governing principle, the perfectly composed design within which characters and objects are placed. And, as noted, in this context 'placed' becomes 'trapped', the perfection of the design serving as the illustration and the expression of Lang's sense of Fatalism. If, with Ophuls, the 'tracks, dollys and camera movements [are] constantly holding out the promise that in passing . . . the look may find its object of desire' (Willemen), then one might say that with Lang the look does not have the chance to seek such an object. Rather, an object (often exactly that) is prescribed, fixed and placed for it. The extent to which the visual pleasure afforded by the Lang-text, and its meaning, is dependent upon design rather than movement is illustrated (literally) by the frame stills which accompany this chapter and which clearly serve not just as illustrations but are ripe with 'significance', with 'meaning', a visual discourse which parallels the written one in a manner which would simply not be possible with Ophuls' work. To freeze Ophuls' flow of flowing images in this way would clearly be working against the grain of the text, where movement is all.

Perhaps the commonest camera movement in the Lang-text is the move back from a close-up of an object or objects to a composition which (re)places the content of the image in a wider context. The emphasis is precisely on what is shown/seen, and the significance of the latter is increased as a result of the camera movement. Paul Joannides, in his article 'Aspects of Fritz Lang' *(Cinema,* nos. 6 & 7), cites a simple example: 'The opening shot of *Ministry of Fear* is a close-up of a clock. The camera slowly draws back to reveal Ray Milland sitting facing it. A sense of subjection is established by this single shot of his life dominated by something outside himself.' What is instantly established is a kind of phenomenology with its denial. The object is displayed for itself, stressed, fills the image, but its significance is then placed within the context of the narrative design as a whole by the move back. There is a sense in which an opposition is established here between the display of the object in close-up and the progression of the narrative. When it moves, Lang's camera traverses the gap between these two poles, and therefore emphasises the narrative process as a substitute for the look/object relation in its 'pure form'. Or, to be more precise, the latter is contained within, and repressed by the mechanism of the former. Ophuls' camera movements are a kind of joy ride for the gaze; they work against the strict pressure of narrativity, offering a pleasure that can, to a degree, be distinguished from it, a game of find the lady. Lang, by contrast, offers a form of repression — the camera movement constantly locks the spectator's gaze into the narrative moment/movement, but the desired object of the gaze within the narrative is very often subject to the repressions, substitutions, displacements, etc., which I have mentioned.

Camera movement: the opening shot of *The Ministry of Fear*

If a pattern emerges from these notes it can perhaps be summarised as follows. At every point where Ophuls' cinema can be read as the 'dramatisation of repression, where the repressed returns and imprints its mark on the representation', Lang's cinema resists, represses and distorts that return. In critical writing on the Lang-text, the marks of that resistance, repression and distortion have traditionally been read as evidence of a vague, undefined fatalism which, in turn, becomes what the narratives are 'about'. But this is to say nothing. *All* narrative is fatalistic, because all narrative consists of described and depicted events, scenes and characters arranged in a certain sequence. To see the weakness of the notion of Fate as a governing principle one need only consider that Lang's characters are always described as being 'trapped' by something. But when has a character within a narrative ever been 'free' (i.e. not trapped) within the sequence/pattern/arrangement which is that narrative? The terms, and therefore the question, are essentially meaningless.

Rather than asking 'What are these films about?' and answering 'Fate', it might be more profitable to instigate a reading of individual narratives within the Lang-text centring on the problematic female presence which, as I have suggested, seems to be a feature of that text. This necessary movement, from the consideration of textual tendencies, moments and symptoms to a consideration of individual narratives, can be compared to Raymond Bellour's idea that the examination of Lang's work with counter-shots reveals that 'at the film's other extreme, as it were, Lang this time plays the counter game against the script'.

A convenient starting point is *Destiny* (*Der müde Tod*). Convenient because one cannot really discuss the film without introducing the terms which recur across the previous pages: destiny, desire, death, the woman as 'problem', the look, and indeed narrative itself. The meta-narrative of the film works to place a young couple under the sign of death (here, crucially, an actual/represented, allegorical male figure within the text). Within this meta-narrative are contained three separate tales which show Death triumphing over the lovers in various times and places. The movement of the film is from a joke about desire and being watched (the embarrassed lovers, in a carriage, placing a cover over a duck's head so that it cannot look at them) to the image of the figure of Death standing over the lovers' united, dead bodies, gazing into the area of camera/ spectator space. It is important that the power of Death is ultimately signified as a tyranny embodied in the look which disturbs the usually sacrosanct area of that space.

In fact, the text establishes an ironic hierarchy of 'looks', which means that although other figures within the narrative(s) are granted looks at the camera, and are made the subject of point of view shots, this is only under the ultimate sway of the look of Death, which signifies triumph over forbidden desire, and hence narrative closure. The gaze of the Girl is thus significantly associated with hallucination, as at the inn, where her look out of frame is followed by a close-up, from her point of view, of a glass of beer which turns into an hour glass, marked by the skeleton shadow of Death's staff. Later, by the wall surrounding Death's plot of land, she again looks out of frame, this time to see the apparitions which pass through the wall. The 'impotence' of her gaze is marked by the shot of her falling on her knees, imploring the apparitions to speak to her. The ultimate irony of the film is that the 'motor' of the three narratives within the framing narrative is literally illusory, a hallucination: a close-up, from the Girl's point of view, of the pages of a book, from which all the words disappear except for the line 'Love is strong as Death'. This is followed by a shot of the Girl gazing at the camera/spectator. The film unfolds precisely in order to discredit the assumed 'authority' of her look, and the message associated with it. What the framed stories repeatedly assert is that 'Love is (not as) strong as Death'. The repression of the 'not as' from the framing story is exactly the term under which the framed narratives are allowed to take place, constantly offering the possibility of the transgression of the Law, a transgression that is repeatedly dealt with, enabling the meta-narrative finally to close.

Two points should be stressed. First, the representation of the woman is not problematic here, in the ways described above. She is an active protagonist, occupying the place held by male figures in almost all of Lang's later films. Secondly, there is no equivalent of the figure of Death

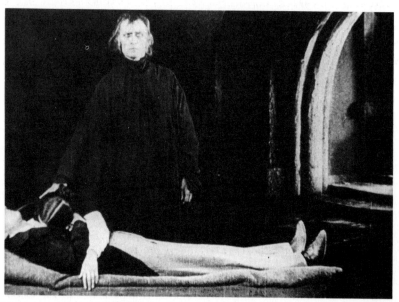

Tyranny of the gaze: *Destiny*

64

in any other Lang film. These two points are vitally linked. The represented figure of Death is essentially a mirror image, within the text, of the place of the spectator (gazing out at the spectator, who gazes back at him . . .). Stephen Neale, in his book *Genre* (British Film Institute 1980), describes mainstream narrative as 'a mode of signification which works constantly to produce coherence in the subject through and across the heterogeneity of the effects that it mobilises and structures. Specifying its effects as narrative functions, pulling these functions into figures of symmetry and balance, mainstream narrative binds together, implicating the subject as the point where its binding mechanisms cohere, the point from where the deployment and configuration of discourses makes "sense".' Death in *Destiny* is the representation of that point. The spectator's position of 'control', of 'mastery', with regard to the narrative is thus actually inscribed into the text.

But this emphatic mirroring of the place of the spectator as the place where the narrative coheres, the point from which it is mastered, is only one function of the figure of Death. Death not only signifies this function but is also the visible guarantee of the satisfaction of the two subjective 'wants' with which every narrative engages: 'the want for the pleasure of process, and the want for the pleasure of its closure' (Neale, op. cit.). Process is guaranteed by Death's offer of repeated chances to save the young man's threatened life, each chance being the trigger for another narrative to unfold. Closure is guaranteed by Death's presence, role and meaning. *Destiny* can thus be read as a text which addresses itself to, and represents, the process, not of destiny, but of narrativity itself. And it is because the content of each episode is thus framed, closed off, made safe for the spectator, whose position of control is the 'subject' of the meta-narrative, that the representation of the woman is unproblematic, to the extent that she fulfils a conventionally male function. Female desire can be repeatedly and sadistically shown, attempting what the meta-narrative guarantees to be impossible, i.e the avoidance of death, here synonymous with the avoidance of the termination of narrative, and the fulfilment of illicit desire. The figure of Death clearly also represents, at an extreme, the tyrant father figure of a doomed Oedipal triangle. The Law which is repeatedly challenged and tested by the Girl's desire is as much the Law of the Father, of patriarchy (the Law which dictates the terms and meaning of desire), as it is of Death. This is a crude formulation but *Destiny*, with its heavily allegorical nature, speaks its terms with exceptional directness.

But if in this way one sees the figure of Death as the crucial focal point of the film, then it would seem useful to examine subsequent narratives within the Lang-text in similar terms, precisely because that focal point now disappears from the text. Or does it? According to some accounts of the Lang-text one can construct a chain, centring on the notion of Fate, of which Death is merely the first link. Thus Julian Petley writes: 'Fate

65

takes on many forms in Lang's works; here it takes the form of Death (in basically allegorical terms), later it takes the form of the machinations of master criminals and supermen, or manifests itself in ungovernable psychoses.' In other words, one moves from Death to Doctor Mabuse and then to Beckert (in *M*) or Mark Lamphere (in *Secret Beyond the Door*). However, here I would like to remove the idea of Fate, and look at the line of the Lang-text in terms of breaks and difference, rather than supposed continuity.

It is clear that Lang's German crime films (*Dr Mabuse der Spieler, Spione* and *Testament of Dr Mabuse*) contain characters (Mabuse himself, and Haighi in *Spione*) who *are* equivalent, to a degree, to the figure of Death. They are tyrannical male figures whose actions instigate narratives which threaten the fulfilment of desire, with the latter signified by and embodied in the relations between a young couple. But if one considers the narrative of, first, *Dr Mabuse der Spieler*, then 'difference' is immediately apparent. The film begins with the establishing of Mabuse's gaze as the controlling principle of the narrative. This is signified by the close-up of his watch, seen from his and the spectator's point of view, which links the depictions of his various criminal operations (swindles on the Stock Exchange, forgery, etc.). The power of his gaze is then reasserted specifically in terms of its relation to control over the representation of the female. In the Folies Bergère a triangle is established, of which the three points are first Cara Carozza, who dances on stage (the woman to be gazed at), secondly Hull the industrialist's son, who is in the audience (who gazes at the woman, and hence is Mabuse's potential victim) and thirdly Mabuse himself (who constitutes Hull as the object of his gaze).

The primacy of Mabuse's look within this system is marked in the text by the shot, from his point of view, through opera glasses, of Hull and his companion, where one lens of the glasses is 'cancelled', and the shot becomes an iris in on the two men. This contrasts with an earlier shot of a man looking at the stage through opera glasses, which is followed by a medium close-up of Cara, but without her image being visibly marked as a point of view shot; i.e. the lenses of the glasses are not rendered as frames within the frame, as with Mabuse. Mabuse's attempt at control of (the representation of) the woman for the furtherance of his plot to ensnare Hull (the 'subject' of the narrative) is underlined by the iris in to the heads of Hull and Cara, when they subsequently meet in the hotel (the next stage of the plot). Thus far then, the parallels between Mabuse and Death hold good at a certain level — the equation of power and the gaze in control over the terms of desire. But at the end of the film the equation emphatically collapses. The narrative ends with Mabuse himself fixed as the object of the gaze of the Law, under the signs of madness and blindness. He is seen sitting on the floor with his forged money — the object of a shot from the shared point of view of the police and the spectator — and is finally led away with his gang of blind forgers. The blind men have previously marked, through difference, Mabuse's power in terms of his gaze, i.e. what they lack. Just before this Mabuse's madness has been signified by representations which are 'out of control' — the hallucinations of his former victims which appear before him, particularly the 'ghost' of Cara at whose feet he collapses.

The crucial factor, obviously, is that Mabuse's omnipotence is cancelled out by the introduction of the counter-presence of an alternative version of 'the Law',* the system of legal power, represented here by State Attorney Von Wenk. Narrative in *Destiny* was the repeated depiction of a struggle against an inevitability, which was 'guaranteed' by a visible representative within the text, i.e. Death, the figure of narrativity. Narrative in *Mabuse* is a struggle between two opposing forces, neither of which is 'privileged' to the degree apparent in the case of Death. In fact, shifting the perspective slightly, a feature of the Lang-text which has often been the subject of critical comment is the repeated parallels drawn between the methods and actions of the Law (LS) and those of the underworld. Very basic examples in *Dr Mabuse der Spieler* are the use of disguises, perpetrated by both Mabuse and Von Wenk, or the .intercutting in Part 2 between these characters, both issuing instructions to their 'gangs'. This kind of structuring is normally linked with a supposed Langian world view which, in various ways, investigates the fallibility of the Law (LS). This would account, for example, for the moment when Von Wenk calls on Mabuse, finds him absent, and leaves his card. On returning to his office he finds Mabuse waiting for him, and remarks, 'Strange how our intentions seem to coincide, Doctor'. But what I would stress here is that their intentions most obviously coincide over the body of Countess Told, who is kidnapped by Mabuse at the close of Part I, and rescued by Von Wenk at the end of Part 2. In other words it is desire which governs/structures the movement of the narrative, and the shifting relations within it, and Mabuse is made part of that shifting pattern, rather than, as with Death, placed outside it.

An obvious result is that the basic Oedipal structure of the narrative is doubled, and Mabuse's function within that structure consequently split. Mabuse gains possession of the Countess from her husband, and drives the latter to suicide, but Von Wenk then gains possession of the Countess from Mabuse, who is driven to madness and into the realms of the blind. The splitting of Mabuse's role is marked in various ways. For example, he is the bearer of the name that cannot be spoken: by Cara, when questioned in prison by Countess Told, by Gutmann, the criminal interrogated by Von Wenk, and by Von Wenk himself, who attempts to

*The two systems of power (legal and patriarchal) signified by 'the Law' are crucially interrelated in Lang's work. Sometimes they are distinguishable from each other, hereafter signified in this account by (LS) or (PS), and sometimes not, signified by (LS/ PS).

Mabuse as illusionist (*Dr Mabuse der Spieler*)

utter the name before falling into the hypnotic trance induced by Mabuse. However, this is mirrored by his forbidding the Countess to speak her husband's name, on pain of the latter's death. But the crucial shift is the previously mentioned subject/object of the look split. This is emphatically marked within the text when Mabuse adopts the role of Weltmann, the stage illusionist and hypnotist; a role in which he still asserts his control over the look and representation (the conjuring of the illusion of the Red Indians within the theatre, the gaze at the camera/spectator which precedes the hypnotising of Wenk), but simultaneously becomes heavily marked as the object of the spectator's gaze, by virtue of appearing as a performer on a stage, a spectacle within the spectacle of the text as a whole.

What the narrative sets in motion, centres on, and attempts to resolve is exactly the problem which, according to Laura Mulvey, is posed by the representation of the female figure:

> She (the female figure) also connotes something that the look continually circles around but disavows: the lack of a penis, implying a threat of castration and hence unpleasure. Ultimately the meaning of the woman is sexual difference, the absence of the penis as visually ascertainable, the material evidence on which is based the castration complex essential for the organisation of entrance to the symbolic

order, and the law of the father. Thus the woman as icon, displayed for the gaze and enjoyment of men, the active controllers of the look, always threatens to evoke the anxiety it originally signified ('Visual Pleasure and Narrative Cinema', *Screen*, Autumn 1975).

The function of the woman as both icon for visual pleasure *and* evoker of anxiety is split in the film between, respectively, the figures of Cara and the Countess. Mabuse's downfall is caused by his failure to deal with this contradiction. He sets up Cara as the object of Hull's gaze in order to entrap him, but is himself destroyed through his involvement with the Countess, who is explicitly posited as woman as enigma — when Von Wenk first encounters her at the club, Schramm's, she is known as Lady Passive, whose name nobody knows, and the montage of shots which introduces the club includes an image of a woman dressed as a man. And enigma equals threat. Laura Mulvey describes one of the ways in which the male unconscious escapes from the anxiety evoked by this threat: 'preoccupation with the re-enactment of the original trauma (investigating the woman, demystifying her mystery), counter-balanced by the devaluation, punishment or saving of the guilty object . . . pleasure lies in ascertaining guilt (immediately associated with castration), asserting control and subjecting the guilty person through punishment or forgiveness.' Von Wenk's function with regard to the Countess is to demystify her mystery by conspiratorially aiding her in its preservation. When the Count arrives at Schramm's, Von Wenk turns off the lights so that she can leave unobserved. Her punishment is necessary, however, as the mystery associated with her explicitly turns on the look. As opposed to Cara, who is the woman offered to the male look, the Countess is the woman who looks. She goes to Schramm's to watch others gamble, to 'observe passions released', and when her husband arrives she effects a disturbance of spectator space by her look directed at the camera. The 'guilty object' is punished (by Mabuse who kidnaps her) *and* saved (by Von Wenk in the final rescue). Thus the narrative works to assert doubly the mastery of the Law (LS/PS) over the 'problem' posed by the figure of the woman: to foreground the association of the desire for visual pleasure and the woman as pure object of the look, but at the same time to depict through narrative events the resolution of the anxieties caused by the female figure. Mabuse and Von Wenk do not embody moral values drawn from outside the text and put into question, but function only to permit this process to take place. Hence, from beginning to end, the narrative turns and progresses on the assertion of the power of one gaze as against another: the 'battles of looks' over the gambling table between Hull and Mabuse, and between Mabuse and Von Wenk; the point of view shots marked by an emphatic iris, allowed to both Mabuse and Von Wenk; the association of hallucinations with madness and death.

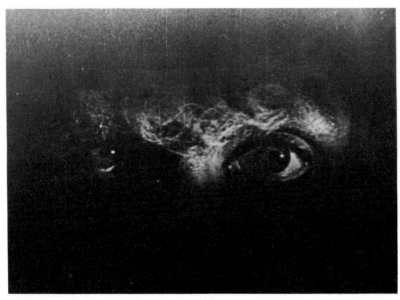

Mabuse's hypnotic gaze (*Dr Mabuse der Spieler*)

What is missing, however, compared to *Destiny*, is the 'unmotivated' gaze at the camera/spectator allowed to the figure of Death. This gaze was on the side of enunciation rather than enounced, and, combined with the film's narrative-as-repetition structure, worked against the naturalisation of the fantasy of the narrative(s). No character in *Dr Mabuse der Spieler* is permitted such a look, but even though looks at the camera are motivated in terms of narrative content (most importantly Mabuse's hypnotic stare) one can see that these shots are marked as 'excessive' in various ways (a close-up of Mabuse's eyes surrounded by darkness, or the camera moving in to a close-up of his face, again framed by blackness). Raymond Bellour suggests that the hypnotic powers ascribed to Mabuse endow him 'with a kind of power in the production of narrative'. I would argue that it is a question of degree and tendency. Bellour's remarks about Mabuse as the enunciator of the narrative are more applicable to the figure of Death in *Destiny*. The introduction of the subject of hypnosis into the text can be read as a stage of displacement, moving the narrative towards *histoire* rather than *discours*, in that Mabuse is not strictly speaking an enunciator, but is firmly embedded in the narrative events. He is balanced by another character (Von Wenk) and is caught up in the drama turning on desire and the female, rather than standing outside those events, as does Death. But at the same time the representation of hypnosis does privilege the power of the gaze, and *suggests* the place of enunciation which lies outside the text. To a degree

Haighi's 'unmotivated' gaze (*Spione*)

the text is thus 'denaturalised'.

Spione can usefully be read as a more acute version of this process. Lang has described the difference between the figures of Mabuse and Haighi, the villain of *Spione*, as follows: 'Dr Mabuse . . . shows, at least in one episode of his criminal career . . . something like a human trait . . . Haighi the master spy is nothing less than what we could call today a human computer . . . Haighi has no human feelings whatsoever.' Mabuse's 'human trait' is his desire for the Countess; the fact that Haighi exhibits no such desire means that he occupies a different position from Mabuse with regard to the events of the narrative. Which is not to suggest that he is outside the narrative content, but rather that the assertion of his presence, and in particular his gaze, as the trigger for events, the point of enunciation, is more marked and sustained. He is at once the figure who through his machinations posits the inevitable problem of the narrative (the investigation of the female), and whose presence becomes intolerable when that problem has been worked through and contained.

The opening scenes of the film juxtapose the power of the looks of Tremaine, the secret agent, and Haighi, but they are established in very different ways. Tremaine is both he who is seen, as unproblematic object of the spectator's gaze, and he who sees (through) the disguise of the spy he unmasks in the office of Burton Jason, head of the secret service. Haighi, however, is only gradually revealed to the gaze of the spectator.

71

The montage of events with which he is connected (the theft of copies of secret documents, the taking of the copy of the coded telegram sent by Tremaine, the complaint made to Jason by the Minister of the Interior) is interspersed with shots of Haighi. He is seen first from behind, secondly from the side and slightly behind, and finally full face on. This process culminates with the arrival of Morrier, the condemned murderer whom Haighi has rescued from the scaffold. He gazes at and approaches Haighi, whose look is identified at this point with that of the camera and the spectator, and there follows a cut to a shot of the man collapsing at Haighi's feet. Haighi's gaze into camera/spectator space is sometimes linked to the gaze of another character within the text (Sonja, at the Café Danielle, looks out of frame, which is followed by a shot, from her point of view, of Haighi, and his nurse, looking at her/the camera/the spectator); but it can also appear to be unplaced in this way, as with the shots of him which are inserted at crucial moments in his plots, for example when the duplicitous Kitty rushes into the arms of Masimoto, whose suicide she will cause, or when Sonja wakes up immediately after the depiction of the train crash in which Tremaine is involved. These shots are clearly intended to assert repeatedly Haighi's role within the narrative, to insert into the scenes the image of the person 'behind the scenes', but their status is problematic simply because they assert the presence of a gaze which refers only to spectator space, and is not bound into the looks of other characters, within and across the space of the image. Consequently they *suggest* enunciation, and *discours* rather than *histoire*.

This tendency is complemented by the status accorded the death of Haighi. His adoption of the role of Nemo the clown, and his appearance on stage, clearly relates to Mabuse's appearance as Weltmann the hypnotist and illusionist, but there is a crucial difference. The presentation of Mabuse as the doubly marked object of the spectator's gaze (spectacle, as performer on stage, within the meta-spectacle of the film as a whole) does not coincide with the closure of the narrative, but is only one step towards it. Mabuse's shifting place within the film's Oedipal trajectory means that the text can end with his depiction as the symbolically castrated object of the gaze of the Law (ps/ls). Haighi, by contrast, is posited as 'outside' the space occupied by those characters (Tremaine, Masimoto, Sonja, Kitty) who act through the crisis caused by the problem of the female, a problem which is instigated by Haighi. Haighi's presence must therefore be 'artificially' inserted at moments of acute crisis, as in the shots mentioned above. By the film's end he has left the wheelchair he occupied and physically entered the space of the acting out of the symbolic drama. But the narrative has solved the problem, in a way I will discuss, which means that Haighi's presence is both unnecessary and impossible. It is unnecessary because he has been replaced by Burton Jason, the acceptable face of patriarchy, whom we see united with Tremaine and Sonja, standing in the wings of the stage,

The death of Haighi/Nemo (*Spione*)

in a shot from Haighi's point of view. It is impossible because it is the reassertion of the motor of the narrative. The narrative can only, and must, terminate with Haighi's removal. Therefore his suicide signals the close of the filmic spectacle and system (he shoots himself while gazing at the camera/spectator and falls to the floor, which is followed by a shot from the stage of the audience applauding, i.e. from the 'impossible' point of view of a dead man), and also the spectacle which occupies the literal 'stage space' within the frame, signified by the final image of the curtains being drawn across the stage. The distinction marked here between a specifically filmic system (based on point of view) and stage space, marked by the two being confused, is an important one. Haighi is associated with a space within the text constructed by montage, edited into scenes but separate from them. His inserted presence disrupts the spatial/linear coherence of the narrative as 'unproblematic' spectacle taking place within the homogeneity of 'theatrical' space. This is not to suggest that the disruption in any way renders the narrative unreadable; but that it is unnecessary and, more important, works against the general movement towards transparency, the tendency to render narrative as *histoire*.

Coupled with this is a tendency to undermine the equation of filmic representation and truth within the represented content/spectacle of the film. This works at several levels. At the most basic level of plot there is a great deal of play around the idea of disguise and multiple identity —

73

Masimoto and the ghosts (*Spione*)

characters are not just who they 'seem to be'. There is also hallucination — the problematic status of elements within the image which are linked with the subjective vision of a character. For example, the three 'ghosts' of dead couriers who appear in front of Masimoto just before he commits suicide, first established as the object of a shot from his point of view, then constituting *him* as the object of their point of view shot, and finally, contradicting their status as his 'fantasy', seen 'objectively' in frame with him. There is both the 'layering' of the image content, part of the rhetoric of silent film, for example the Japanese flag which is superimposed on the image after Masimoto has discovered that the secret treaty has been stolen, or the number 3313 seen over train wheels before Tremaine's crash; and its converse, where the visual surface of the image is stripped away to reveal an alternative 'truth', as in the shot of a vase which becomes 'transparent' so that the microphone concealed within it can be revealed. The male image is often doubled in the form of a trace, as with Tremaine's fingerprints, or the handprint he leaves on a chair in his hotel. The shadows of two men are seen struggling on a wall behind the bound figure of Sonja. There is an emphasis on photography, in terms of threat. Thus Tremaine discovers a camera hidden in the lapel of the spy he unmasks in Jason's office; he leafs through photographs of dead agents; Haighi shows photographs of Tremaine and Masimoto to Sonja and Kitty respectively, before dispatching them to ensnare their victims; Haighi's imminent downfall is signalled by his image being displayed on a 'wanted' poster. A striking image is a shot, from Haighi's point of view, of a photograph of Tremaine, seen gradually coming into focus through a magnifying glass through which he is looking.

One can argue that what is being constantly 'dramatised' and 'displayed' in all these examples is the basic fetishistic structure of the cinematic signifier itself. This has been described by Stephen Neale as follows: 'The cinematic signifier is perceptually present, but it nevertheless exists as a trace of absence . . . the very status of the cinematic signifier inaugurates a "splitting of belief", the regime of credence that can be characterised as "I know very well and yet" (I know this is only cinema, and yet it is so "present" . . .)'. The regime of credence, in which mainstream narrative cinema clearly places a massive investment, is undercut by what Raymond Bellour describes as the 'inventory of maps, plans, letters, photographs, all the multifarious pointers which blaze a trail through Lang's forty films'. These form a series of images of which the content, constantly and emphatically, refers to that which lies outside, to that which does not meet the eye, of which they are signs. Hence the significance of the 'secret treaties', false and otherwise, around which the narrative of *Spione* turns and progresses; they are pure fetish objects, their content remains unspoken.

The importance of the versions of fetishism noted above is that they lead to the real 'point' of the narrative, the solving of the mystery of the female, and the fear she arouses. Laura Mulvey describes the second of

The vase concealing a microphone (*Spione*)

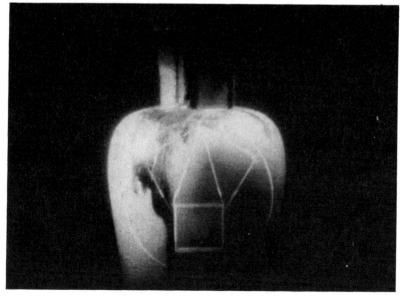

Tremaine's image under the magnifying glass (*Spione*)

the 'two avenues of escape from this castration anxiety [as] the complete disavowal of castration by the substitution of a fetish object or turning the represented figure itself into a fetish so that it becomes reassuring rather than dangerous'. A combination of these two processes is depicted in the relationship between Tremaine and Sonja. However, the castration anxiety aspect is stressed by the parallel relationship between Masimoto and Kitty. The two couplings are initially linked through irony. After Sonja has left Tremaine at the Café Danielle we see him with Masimoto. Tremaine is drinking heavily and becomes hysterical when Masimoto tells him he is 'the victim of a beautiful spy', and that agents should be 'wary of women'. The irony works against Masimoto in two ways. First, the spectator has already seen Sonja telling Haighi that she loves Tremaine, and Haighi threatening to keep her as a prisoner as a result. Also, Masimoto's warning about women is followed by a cut to Sonja and a shot, from her point of view, of Tremaine's identity card, which she presses against her face — a clear pointer to the fetishistic solution to the problem. Masimoto's wisdom is thus undercut through montage. Secondly, we see Haighi setting Kitty on Masimoto's trail, and the latter finding her on the street at night. Difference then becomes apparent: Kitty is emphatically established as the woman who signifies fear of castration for the male, under the Law of the Father. Masimoto discovers that Kitty has stolen the treaty, and as a result commits

76

hara-kiri by slitting open his stomach. This is intercut with the image of Haighi tossing Kitty a necklace as her reward. By contrast Tremaine turns to a fetish object, the madonna and child medallion which Sonja has given to him, with the words 'May it always bring you luck'. The specifically fetishistic significance of the medallion becomes crudely manifest when Tremaine is shown making it the object of his gaze (it is seen in a shot from his point of view), and then rubbing it, with a look which signifies yearning. The fact that he then throws the medallion to the ground is a melodramatic sign of the threat of the situation becoming pathological, according to Freud's definition in *Three Essays on Sexuality*: 'when the longing for the fetish passes beyond the point of being merely a necessary condition attached to the sexual object and actually takes the place of the normal aim, and, further, when the fetish becomes detached from a particular individual and becomes the sole sexual object.' The purpose of the narrative is precisely to disavow this pathological fetishism, to replace the madonna with the 'real' Sonja, once the threat of castration has been worked through via Masimoto and Kitty. The replacement occurs during the attempt to kill Tremaine by means of the engineered train crash. Just before his carriage is hit by the oncoming train he wakes up and looks at the medallion. The crash itself is followed by a cut to Sonja waking up and realising the significance of the number 3313. And once Tremaine has been rescued from the wreckage Sonja can be transformed into woman as victim to be saved, rescued from the clutches of Haighi by Tremaine. The fetishisation of the (already, by its cinematic nature, fetishistic) figure of Sonja, and its disavowal, enables the narrative to conclude with the assertion of the Law of the Father, but with this law now seen as benevolent. Haighi is removed and replaced by Burton Jason. The depiction of the Jason/Tremaine/Sonja group as the object of Haighi's gaze is the signal for his suicide, the problem of the woman, of which he is the instigator, having been worked through.

Tzvetan Todorov has suggested, about the construction of narrative, that: 'The minimal complete plot consists in the passage from one equilibrium to another. An "ideal" narrative begins with a stable situation which is disturbed by some power or force. There results a state of disequilibrium; by the action of a force directed in the opposite direction, the equilibrium is re-established; the second equilibrium is similar to the first but the two are never identical' ('The Grammar of Narrative' in *The Poetics of Prose*, Cornell University Press 1977). In the early crime films, as discussed above, the sense of disequilibrium hung on two related factors. First, woman as mystery, the visible site of male fears; and secondly, the presence within the text of male figures whose machinations provoked the eruption of those fears. In *Testament of Dr*

Testament of Dr Mabuse: the containment of Mabuse's image . . .

Mabuse this is no longer the case. The central male/female relationship, between Tom and Lilli, is threatened, but unproblematic as regards her status. Precisely the opposite: it is Tom who is torn between the underworld and the Law (LS/PS), who moves from under the sign of the former to the latter, who is the 'problem'. Consequently, and very noticeably, there is no need for the splitting of the female function, as with Cara/the Countess in *Dr Mabuse der Spieler* and Kitty/Sonja in *Spione*. Lilli embodies the idea of the female firmly contained and functioning within the Law (LS/PS). This is doubly stressed when she and Tom are first shown together in a restaurant. First, there is a flashback which reveals that Lilli is an employee of the Labour Exchange. She mediates between the Law (LS) and he who is marked as outside it (the unemployed man to whom she lends money). Secondly, when Tom asks her if she has ever been in love, she leaves embarrassed — she represses the possibility of the female as subject of desire. She functions as object of desire in order to help define Tom's position as regards the Law (LS/PS).

Much more problematic is the play around the presence/absence of the figure of Mabuse. The sense of equilibrium depends precisely on his being contained, described and depicted by the Law (LS) to which he poses a threat. Hence the scene of the lecture given by Dr Baum, head of the asylum in which the mad Mabuse is incarcerated. It is not only his image which is frozen, contained in a slide showing his face framed

78

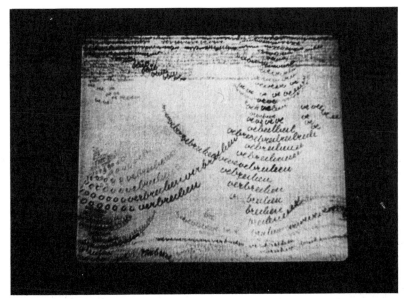

. . . and of his discourse

within the frame, but also, specifically, his discourse. Another slide shows paper covered with scribbled writings, while Baum's voice over describes how words, then sentences, then detailed plans for crimes appeared in turn. Also mentioned is the repression of his voice from the soundtrack, as Baum tells how Mabuse has not spoken since he was locked up. Equilibrium is thus threatened by the possibility of Mabuse the enunciator, of physical presence and voice coming together in order to initiate narrative in the form of crime. The narrative of the film's present thus concerns itself with the fear of this possibility.

Sound and image tracks are symptomatically rendered as 'problematic' in the film's opening. Hofmeister, the ex-policeman on the trail of Mabuse's gang, is seen crouched, listening to the mysterious pounding noise of machinery which dominates the soundtrack. A little later he looks out of a window, and there is a high angle shot of a lorry below. This is then revealed to be *not* the point of view shot which classical editing would lead one to expect, as the lorry is seen to pull away and Hofmeister emerges from a door below, in the same shot. This kind of visual/aural 'disturbance' is then linked specifically with Mabuse, as Hofmeister attempts to phone through his information to Inspector Lohmann. At the moment he is about to utter Mabuse's name the image goes completely black. Hofmeister's cry of 'The lights have gone out', and his appeal to Lohmann for help, is followed by the sound of gunshots, with the darkness being punctuated by flashes of light.

Hofmeister's subsequent madness is thereafter signified by his inability to plug the gap in the soundtrack which should be filled by the name 'Mabuse'. His final speaking of that name coincides with Dr Baum, by now possessed by the 'spirit' of Mabuse, taking his place in a cell in the asylum.

This is paralleled on the image track by the taboo among the members of Mabuse's gang about 'wanting to see the man behind the curtain', a desire which, as a flashback reveals, brings only death. For his gang Mabuse exists primarily on the soundtrack, his visual presence being reduced to a shadow seen through a curtain. And this in turn is revealed to be the image of a cut-out wooden figure when Tom finally does burst through that curtain. At one point, during an interrogation, Lohmann states that he wants to know the name of 'the man in the dark, the man behind the scenes'. This is followed by a derisory cut to a shot of the wooden 'Mabuse', sinking under the waters in the flooded room where Tom and Lilli have been trapped. His question is finally answered, in the same tone, by Hofmeister who, as he is led from his cell, tells Lohmann, 'The man is called Mabuse'. The man to whom he is referring is in fact Dr Baum, who has just said to Hofmeister: 'May I introduce myself? My name is Dr Mabuse.' The ending of the film is deliberately similar to, but significantly different from, those of its predecessors. The threat to the Law (LS/PS) is contained, as Baum is constituted as the object of the combined gazes of Lohmann and Kent. But whereas Mabuse and Haighi were also made the stressed object of the gaze of the spectator, Baum is established as that which is repressed from the image track. The gaze at him is signified by the look directed by Lohmann/Kent at the spectator/Baum/the camera. This look is repeated by the attendant who closes the door of the cell in the film's final shot. The Law does not triumph here but emphatically denies and represses. As Lohmann says to Kent: 'Come on, this is no longer a police job.' 'Mabuse' cannot be contained — the idea of him, now embodied within Baum, must be removed/repressed from the image track, in order that the narrative may close.

Lohmann's desire to know 'the name' is a simplification and a misreading of what that name signifies, or is signified by, within the text. Lohmann links the name solely to the physical presence, the body of Mabuse. But, ironically, the decipherment of the name 'Mabuse', which Hofmeister has scratched on to a pane of glass, is followed by the revelation that the person Mabuse is now simply a (dead) body. But this does not remove the idea of 'Mabuse' from the text. This is emphasised by the significant pan up to Baum, after the sheet has been pulled down to reveal the face of the dead Mabuse. Mabuse in *Dr Mabuse der Spieler* and Haighi in *Spione* were primarily name-bearing characters. But *Testament of Dr Mabuse* marks a move towards abstraction. Mabuse in this film is not primarily a person. 'Mabuse' is the name that cannot be

Mabuse as shadow (*Testament of Dr Mabuse*)

spoken, a shadow behind a curtain, a voice, a wooden shape, a signature on letters, an image projected on to a screen, a name scratched on to glass, a hallucination. The narrative is driven by the need to discover the physical referent, to which, it is supposed, these signifiers refer. Only when this link is established can equilibrium return. But the chief mark of the narrative's abstraction is that it refuses to privilege such a referent. Narrative is here resolved only by a further signifier/signified split. Baum 'becomes' Mabuse, a link established only in terms of further illusion(ism), as the 'spirit' of Mabuse is seen to enter his body.

The earlier crime films played on the idea of disguise. Part of the task faced by the Law (LS) was to reduce multiple identity to a single character who could then be confined or killed. In *Testament of Dr Mabuse* this is no longer possible; identity means nothing because there is nothing to identify, there is only a plethora of signs. The existence of the latter *as* problematic signs (what is their referent?) is the very crux of the narrative. The 'death' of the narrative occurs when the multiple signifiers of the idea of Mabuse are replaced by the figure of Baum, who becomes the single literal 'embodiment' of that idea, in the manner described above. This notion is suggested earlier in the film. Dr Kramm dies, in the celebrated murder at the traffic lights, after he establishes a link between Mabuse's scribbled plans and the newspaper report of a jewel robbery. Both are seen in the same shot, a close-up from his point of view. The plans, the signs, cease to be problematic when they are linked

81

with — contained within — the newspaper report, with the latter viewed as the reflection of the truth of events in the real world. And death naturally follows . . .

The signs of Mabuse are the threat of the eruption of repressed memories. The disequilibrium of the narrative is the return of a previous disequilibrium, not only in terms of Mabuse, but also with regard to Tom. His association with the underworld is linked with the memory of woman as 'problem'. He reveals to Lilli that he was in prison for killing two people, his sweetheart and his best friend. 'Mabuse' is what ties him to this memory — it is only by acknowledging the Law of the benevolent father (Lohmann) that he can attain Lilli in 'reality'. The alternative is clearly posed. The threat is that she becomes a memory (his letter to her: 'Forget me. I shall never forget you') and a fetishised object (the photograph of her on his desk, revealed to the spectator in close-up).

It might now be useful to flash back to *Metropolis,* an earlier film in a different genre (science fiction rather than thriller), and to consider it in the terms applied to the crime film trilogy described above. It is now a critical commonplace to read the film's ending as a reactionary, humanist resolution of the problems raised by the film. Fredersen, the capitalist ruler of the futuristic city, shakes hands with the workers' foreman; the two are linked by Freder, the ruler's son. What this signifies in terms of 'labour relations' is articulated by Maria, the fourth figure in this 'family group': 'There can be no understanding between the hands and the brain, unless the heart acts as mediator.' Peter Wyeth, in the magazine *North by Northwest,* has written: 'The ideological consciousness expressed in the film is a "reformist" one, which fails to tackle the fundamental causes of the workers' misery, the relations of power in Metropolis, and merely substitutes a more enlightened Fredersen as the solution to the problem.' However, this presupposes that the 'problem' in the film is that of the power relations in Metropolis and the consequent workers' misery. In fact, if one applies Todorov's equilibrium/disequilibrium opposition, then the 'problem' can be read rather differently.

The equilibrium established at the beginning of the film is based precisely on the rigid stratification and division of the classes. The masters live high above the workers' city, which is 'far below the earth'. The initial instance of disequilibrium is the appearance in the masters' pleasure garden, where Freder is seen, of Maria, accompanied by a group of children. It is only when Freder follows Maria and the children that he witnesses the explosion and the loss of life in the machine room, which sends him rushing to confront his father. So one can legitimately read the primary problem of the film as the 'trouble' caused by Freder seeing Maria with the children. This is doubly stressed, first by the cut

The idealised mother: Maria and the children in *Metropolis*

from Freder looking out of frame, to Maria and the children constituted as the object of his gaze in a point of view shot, and secondly by his asking 'Who was that?', rather than 'Who were they?'. Maria has told him that the children are his brothers; one can read his question as evidence that he takes her remark 'literally', in the sense that he posits a familial problem, seeing Maria as an idealised mother figure. I would argue that the film can be productively read in a way which privileges the investigation of the 'problem' caused by the figure of Maria. This links the film to the thrillers, and makes the class conflict a secondary issue which is automatically resolved when the Maria 'trouble' has been worked through.

The threat surrounding the figure of Maria is very explicitly a threat against the Law of the Father. Fredersen dismisses his servant Joseph because he believes that the latter knew of the plans for a workers' uprising. Freder follows Joseph and allies himself with him, but it is Freder's estrangement from his father which is stressed. Freder's words, 'Father, you don't know what it means to be dismissed by you', are followed by a shot showing Fredersen in the front of the frame, back to camera, gazing at Freder, who backs away from the power of that gaze. When Freder catches up with Joseph, there is a cut back to his father looking out of frame. This in turn is followed by a shot, from the latter's point of view, of the doors through which Freder has just passed. In other words what Freder's alliance with Maria and his worker brothers creates is an empty space in terms of the father's gaze, as the object of which he is lost. This is doubly marked as Freder enters the machine room, where he is enveloped in steam, i.e. also obscured as the object of the spectator's gaze. And this is followed by the *assertion* of Freder's gaze, as shots of the machines as obvious spectacle are intercut with shots of him looking. But the denial of patriarchal authority, signified by this simple play around the power of different looks, is depicted as intolerable. The place which Freder finds among his 'brothers' is signified, through religious reference, as that of pain. His cry of 'Father, Father' is linked with the image of him 'crucified' on the hands of the clock-like machine.

In both *Dr Mabuse der Spieler* and *Spione* it was seen that the contradictory aspects of what the female figure signified, basically pleasure and anxiety, were dealt with by splitting the female function between two characters. *Metropolis* copes with the problem through the iconography of the science fiction genre, specifically the figure of the robot, the false Maria. Even before the robot has assumed the identity of Maria's physical double its function is made clear. Rotwang, the inventor, draws back a curtain and the robot is seen, in a shot from Fredersen's point of view, on a pedestal, i.e. marked as the object of the male gaze. But its threatening aspect, as an evocation of the fear of castration, is also stressed. When the robot extends a hand towards Fredersen he backs away, and we learn that Rotwang has actually lost a hand during the creation of the machine.

The introduction of the robot is followed by the workers' meeting called by Maria, where, like the robot, she is objectified in a series of shots from the various points of view of Freder, Fredersen and Rotwang. She is associated with religious connotations, through her name, her image (the madonna, with arms outstretched, surrounded by crosses) and her discourse (the parable of the Tower of Babel which she recounts to the workers) which all, almost parodically, strengthen the notion of her as idealised mother. One can also at this point see the role of father as tyrant being displaced on to Rotwang, as Fredersen instructs him to produce the robot in the likeness of Maria, which he will use to destroy the workers' faith in her. It is thus specifically Rotwang who will be associated with the female figure posed as threat, which will enable Fredersen to be represented as the *benevolent* patriarchal figure at the conclusion of the film — a similar strategy to that adopted in *Spione* with the figures of Haighi and Burton Jason. The threat which Maria represents is now marked specifically in terms of the power of her gaze, under the sway of which Freder is placed. She is no longer simply the object of his look but very pointedly gazes back at and down on him. A shot of Maria looking down at Freder, who has his back to the camera/spectator, is balanced by a slightly high angle shot from behind her, which shows him gazing up at her face. She then kisses him, and he closes his eyes in ecstasy. Freder then leaves, with Maria's promise to meet him in the cathedral, the promise of the fulfilment of desire. But Rotwang intervenes to thwart this promise, to prevent Freder gaining access to the object of his Oedipal desires, and the perspective instantly shifts. Maria's gaze is denied, it cannot find its object. Rotwang is seen to drop a stone, which is followed by a shot, from Maria's point of view, of the empty space where he 'should' be. The power of Rotwang's look is then stressed, with the torch beam which pins Maria against a door as she tries to escape him. She is marked as the threat of death, a shot of skulls being followed by a close-up of her face. For her place within the patriarchal power structure to be reasserted she must be shown as not simply depicted but contained. Hence the image of her screaming, seen from above through the glass in the roof of Rotwang's dwelling. The image is then 'doubled' by the shot of her body encased in glass, as the robot assumes her identity. This scene also doubles the shot of her trapped in the beam of Rotwang's torch, as her body and the robot are seen surrounded by beams and circles of light during the transformation.

From this point, the 'real' Maria can no longer be the object of Freder's desire. The narrative jokily depicts the consequence of her remaining so, a lapse into fetishism signified by the piece of cloth from her dress which Freder finds as he searches for her. By means of the figure of the robot Maria, Freder is forced back under the sway of the Law of the Father, the law which dictates the terms by which he must view Maria. Hence the shot, from Freder's point of view, of the robot and

Metropolis: Maria trapped by the torch beam

his father together, he touching her/its shoulder. Freder's rejection of this image, signified by hallucination, distortion and 'interference' on the image track, and his subsequent collapse, occasions the representation of the ultimate threat which accompanies the depiction of Maria as *attainable* object. The robot Maria is seen as the object of the collective gaze of a roomful of men, the test of whether she is 'real' or not. She is represented as 'pure' image, illuminated in silhouette. A series of cuts follows: from Freder sitting up in bed and opening his eyes, to Maria dancing on the pedestal, to the watching men. The last shot then dissolves into a sea of eyes. This mark of excess, after a cut back to Freder, is then doubled, as the men rush the pedestal, reaching up to touch Maria. The link suggested by the editing between the depiction of the test and the 'projection' of Freder's desire is then made firm by his hallucination of the figures of the Seven Deadly Sins, which he had examined in the cathedral while waiting for Maria. After a shot of a tower in the city shooting forth beams of light, the figure of Death, in the guise of the Grim Reaper, advances towards Freder/the camera/ spectator, swinging its scythe. And under this (to say the least) emphatic sign of the threat of castration, Freder collapses back on to the bed.

Once the idea of Maria as object of desire has been associated with the threat of castration, the text works to remove the robot Maria, now rendered superfluous. This is achieved by a process of balance and opposition. The rebelling workers turn on the robot Maria when they believe she has caused the deaths of their children, through the destruction she has unleashed. Conversely, the 'real' Maria is acknowledged as such by Freder when he sees her as the saviour of those children. The figures of the children reaching up to her replace the lusting men in the earlier scene. The distinction is underlined as the workers burn the robot, and the figure is stripped of its clothing. The possibility of the female form being revealed as signifier of castration is repressed by the flames which consume the body at the moment of that revelation. And as the body is stripped, Freder rejects the image, and turns to see Rotwang threatening the figure of the 'real' Maria. In the ensuing struggle between Freder and Rotwang, the latter is killed. This is the final requirement for the return of equilibrium, since Rotwang's presence, once the robot Maria has been rendered 'unnecessary', threatens the image of Fredersen as benevolent patriarch, which the narrative works finally to establish. Thus Fredersen's cry of 'Save my son', as Freder fights with Rotwang, is indicative of the threat posed to his power by the presence of Rotwang. This has been marked earlier when, at the height of the chaos, Fredersen is seen in his office asking 'Where is my son?', as patterns of light play over the walls, a further flashback to the signifier of Rotwang's power, the beam of light from the torch.

The sense of equilibrium restored is embodied in the relations

86

The Grim Reaper (*Metropolis*)

established by the final image. Maria has ceased to be the object of investigation by Freder; the threat to the Law of the Father posed by that investigation has been worked through. She has been 'punished', through her experience with Rotwang, and 'saved' by Freder, an experience analogous to that undergone by the Countess in *Dr Mabuse der Spieler* and Sonja in *Spione* (the idea of kidnapping being common to all three films). Her only function at the end of *Metropolis* is to speak the Law of the Father, while representing the image of the idealised mother (signified by her saving the children), which is crucial for the maintenance of the Law. Freder 'refinds' his place as regards the benevolent father and the idealised mother; and, at the end of his Oedipal trajectory, assumes his role as a function of the patriarchal, oppressive order. The figures within the text who are associated with 'excess' (the robot Maria, site of male fears, and Rotwang, father as tyrant) have been removed.

These accounts of examples of Lang's German work are deliberately reductive. It is usually the 'variety' of these films which is stressed. Thus *Dr Mabuse der Spieler* reflects the decadence of Germany after the First World War. *Spione* is a masterpiece of complex narrative weave. *Testament of Dr Mabuse* is a thinly disguised picture of the Hitler menace. *Metropolis* is a brilliantly imagined and realised picture of an oppressive futuristic society (exactly what is missing from my account). But if one tracks inward rather than outward, then these descriptions of the films seem to be concealing a core of interest which repeatedly links the process of narrative and the investigation of the woman as Other. When this latter point is avoided, as in *Testament of Dr Mabuse,* then there is a tendency towards a kind of abstraction. Signification itself becomes the problematic object of the narrative's investigation. The investigation of 'female trouble' is always within the confines of a very overt Oedipal trajectory, which has as its end point the emphatic assertion of the patriarchal 'family group', core of the Law, as equilibrium. Obviously central to this repeated story are the tyrant figures, near enunciators, subjects of the controlling gaze. But also, vitally, precisely the figures who now disappear from the Lang-text, with the passage to America. They do re-emerge, but in a 'naturalised' form: the difference between, for example, Mabuse and Mike Lagana, the gangster in *The Big Heat.* What is important is that the American counterparts do not aspire to the point of enunciation. Exceptions, proving the rule, are the newspaper chiefs, Walter Kyne (in *While the City Sleeps*) and Austin Spencer (in *Beyond a Reasonable Doubt*). They instigate stories (catch the Lipstick Killer; disprove the 'truth' of circumstantial evidence) for their newspapers which then largely comprise the filmic narratives. But the fact that they *are* placed as newspaper owners by the filmic meta-narratives of course justifies their aspirations in narrative terms.

It must be stressed, however, that the investigation of the 'female trouble' does not cease in the American films. The Oedipal pattern is subject to various forms of naturalisation, disguise and displacement (of the kind mentioned above); it becomes more covert, but it remains. In this sense the text does not develop and cohere. Rather it is marked by difference (the differences between individual films, the differences between the German and American periods), but difference can usefully be read as strategies evolved for disguising an essential obsessive core, for working potentially endless variations upon it. *You Only Live Once* provides a clear example of this process. The film opens with the mark of the Law (LS). A shot of a building inscribed with the words 'Hall of Justice' is followed by a cut to a sign on a door which reads 'Public Defender'. Eddie Taylor is being released from prison, and Jo, who works for Whitney, the Public Defender, is going to join him. Later, in the prison, the Warden tells Eddie that he is being released thanks to Whitney's efforts. The ostensible message of the film, the way in which it is usually read, is that Jo and Eddie are finally destroyed not through the malevolence of the Law but through the exposure of its fallibility, via a series of coincidences. This is seen as the work of Fate, dealing with Eddie the 'three time loser'. But at the same time a clear counter-movement is established. When the District Attorney asks Whitney if Jo is still in love with Eddie, Whitney's 'Yes' is marked by a cut to a shot of him from a slightly raised angle. And subsequently, as Whitney and Father Dolan watch Jo and Eddie leave the prison together, Dolan remarks that he knows how Whitney 'feels about Jo', and that it is no wonder he thinks she has made the wrong decision. Whitney's function as regards the Law as legal system is to reinforce the image of that Law as fallible but benevolent, not responsible for Eddie's fate. But this is incompatible with the Oedipal pattern established around the characters of Whitney, Jo and Eddie, whereby the couple's desire for each other is complicated by the involvement of Whitney. Eddie's release from the custody of the Law (LS) means that he is allowed access to Jo, the object of his desire, outside the terms of the Law (PS). The figure of Whitney is bound into both systems, and it is the resulting dilemma that the narrative attempts to solve. It does so later through the figure of Father Dolan. The split between Whitney/Dolan is the modified equivalent of the splits in the German films. Here, however, it occurs not in terms of benevolent/tyrannical, because this option is withdrawn by the removal of the unproblematic opposition between law and crime, which structured the German thrillers. Father Dolan can be seen as an almost pure 'device' which permits a form of closure.

Eddie Taylor's move from prison to the outside world is marked as a shift from a pre-Oedipal phase of bisexuality based on sexual misrecognition, here suggested by 'confusion', to the discovery of the truth concerning the status of the female. Before Eddie is united with Jo he leaves behind his cellmate, who offers him the socks he has washed for him and strikes a caricatured female pose as he asks Eddie to send him a picture of a movie star with 'big blue eyes'. Significantly, he then warns Eddie to beware of women, who will drive him 'fruitcake'. As Eddie moves towards Jo the shift is emphasised by the tracking shot, from Eddie's point of view, which ends in a close-up of her face, gazing at the camera/spectator/Eddie. Eddie's momentary identification with the subject of the filmic discourse, constituting Jo as the frozen object of his active gaze, is significantly counterbalanced by the plethora of representations and traces of both him and Jo which occur throughout the text, effectively marking the journey to death. One can cite his record card seen in a shot from the warden's (Law's) point of view, his picture in the Valley Tavern owner's detective magazine, their reflections in the pool of water with the frogs, his initials on the hat found by the police (the hat itself shown in a newspaper photograph), the three possible newspaper headlines describing the possible results of his trial ('Taylor Freed in Massacre', 'Taylor Jury Deadlocked', 'Taylor Guilty'), the shot of him being filmed by newsreel cameras as he is led from the court after being found guilty, the wanted poster by which Jo is recognised as she buys cigarettes shortly before they are killed. All this culminates in the shot of the couple seen through the telescopic sight of the policeman's rifle at the moment of death (when they are 'shot').

Sexual confusion: Eddie Taylor and cellmate (*You Only Live Once*)

That Eddie cannot ultimately be allowed access to Jo outside the patriarchal order and its terms is in fact insisted on at the moment when he fixes her with his gaze. She is seen behind, and separated from him by, the prison bars. This moment is rhymed by the shot, from Eddie's point of view, of Jo seen through the window of their home, when he returns after the robbery. She is visible, graspable, but behind glass. Their union is henceforth denied by the Law (LS/PS), the escape from which had allowed its possibility. Almost immediately after this moment Eddie is arrested. In fact their 'idyll' is marked as at once regressive (the frogs which remind Eddie of his childhood), idealised (Jo compares the frogs to Romeo and Juliet), illusory (their reflections seen in the pond) and irrational (Jo decides they fell in love because she was 'mixed up'). And finally it is impossible because it relies on a false assumption of transcendent subjectivity ('What do we care about anybody?' remarks Jo as they leave the Valley Tavern) which is constantly denied by the textual strategy of repeatedly doubling and stressing their objectified represented presence.

And just as the Law (LS) constitutes Eddie as the object of its discourse, so it is precisely because the status of that discourse as truth is called into question that the Law (PS) pulls Eddie (and Jo) back within its jurisdiction. The Law (LS) is fallible because it relies on verisimilitude, what seems to be true. The *text* indicates clearly that the filmic discourse's status as representation renders verisimilitude prob-

The object of desire — fixed but barred (*You Only Live Once*)

lematic. Eddie's hat, bearing his initials, is seen in close-up on a bedside table. The camera gaze moves from the hat, across pictures of Jo, to the figure of a man lying on the bed. But the man is not Eddie, as the progress of the shot suggests, because Eddie is then seen gazing out of the window. The robbery scene then similarly plays on the notion of confusion over who or what is seen — eyes framed in the rear window of a car, a face hidden behind a gas mask, again the hat bearing the initials E.T. These images climax in the overhead shot of the street clouded by gas from the exploding grenades. Eddie's trial and conviction indicate the fallibility of the Law (LS). This is then counterbalanced by the discovery of the truth (Eddie's innocence) at the moment of his attempted jail break. However, the truth can only be represented to him through a sign-system, the telegraph message that he has been pardoned, which he refuses to read. Eddie's refusal to read the message reflects what the Law (LS) has itself discovered through his wrongful conviction: that signs do not equal 'truth'. Eddie's subsequent shooting of Father Dolan is customarily read as the culmination of the machinations of an undefined Fate (for example by Julian Petley: 'Eddie Taylor's story is one of the clearest examples of the power of Fate in all of Lang's films'). 'Fate', in other words, is seen as the supreme determining force, the workings of the Law (LS) being as much under its sway as the individual man or woman. However, I would argue that it is not Fate which is seen to triumph but the process of the other Law, that of the patriarchal system of oppressive

91

Alternative versions: *You Only Live Once*

order, and that the fallibility of the legal system serves *its* ends.

The fact that Eddie is pulled back into the custody of the Law (LS) after the robbery, means that the Law (PS) can begin to reassert itself. In the court building Eddie and a policeman are seen emerging from a lift. The camera then pans to the right to reveal Jo and Whitney seated on a bench. When Eddie refuses to speak to Jo, Whitney embraces her. But the order of patriarchy cannot be re-established as simply as this shot suggests. Jo now bears the mark of Eddie's Oedipal transgression — she is to bear his child. The situation demands that they both be punished for equilibrium to be restored. Whitney's remark that 'If he dies it'll just about kill Jo too' ostensibly signifies his concern for her, but can equally be read as an expression of the need for her to be replaced — which she is, by her sister Bonnie, who takes Jo's place within the new familial order. Jo hands over the significantly unnamed baby ('We just call him baby') to Whitney and Bonnie before she leaves to rejoin Eddie in death.

Eddie's punishment takes the form of a joke. Having acted out half of his Oedipal fantasy, and gained possession of the mother, he is punished by the Law (LS) for completing the pattern — he kills the father. The point is made explicit on the soundtrack: 'Stay out of this, Father . . . I'm all washed up, I killed Father Dolan . . . I can still see Father Dolan's face.' This joke on the part of the Law (PS) — the offering of a suitably titled surrogate to be sacrificed in order that patriarchy may assert itself through punishment — is also 'justified' in terms of the Law (ᴌs). The Law was seen to be fallible through the visual confusion marking the robbery. Although Eddie's murder of Father Dolan is marked by a similar 'difficulty of seeing' (the gas from the grenades is replaced by swirling fog) it is unambiguous. There is no doubt that he is seen to shoot the priest.

The murder of Father Dolan marks the convergence of the aims of the two systems signified by the term 'the Law'. Flashing back, one can see that Eddie's attempted escape is rendered as an act of defiance against both systems. In order to gain entrance to the prison hospital, where a gun is concealed, he cuts his wrists. The next shot emphatically dismembers his body, as blood is seen dripping on to the floor between his feet. This occurs after he has been told that he cannot see his wife, the implication being that the Law (ᴌs and ᴘs) can only deny him what he has no fear of: the female body, the castrated status of which he has come to terms with, outside patriarchy. Hence his symbolic acknowledgment of the fact of castration. But his killing of 'the Father' means that his defiance can be 'justifiably' punished by the Law (ᴌs). Both faces of the Law are satisfied but the patriarchal face evades responsibility for the punishment. Whitney actually declares that 'the law', as opposed to himself, must find and kill Eddie, since they, not him, are to blame for what has happened. He cynically assumes a benevolent role, providing Jo with the means, car and money, to rejoin Eddie, but only in the

You Only Live Once: the moment of death

93

knowledge that 'the law' will deal with them, leaving him to be united with the surrogate mother (Bonnie) and child. Order and equilibrium are restored. Eddie's attempt to grasp subjectivity outside the terms of patriarchy is ironically placed by the shot, from his point of view, of light breaking over the woods at the moment of his death. On the soundtrack Father Dolan's voice once again constitutes him as the butt of the Oedipal joke: 'You're free, Eddie. The gates are open.'

In the German films, the two systems signified by the idea of 'the Law' were ultimately placed in opposition to various embodiments of 'evil' (Mabuse, Haighi, Rotwang), that which must be removed for equilibrium to return. The above account attempts to show what happens in *You Only Live Once* when that opposition is removed. The law itself becomes problematic, and strategies (notably the introduction of 'Father' Dolan) must be used to work the problem through, via the inevitable Oedipal trajectory. *You and Me* uses a similar split around what is signified by the Law in order to investigate a rather different terrain, in order to assert that the *economic* equilibrium established at the beginning of the film is dependent on, and intertwined with, the containment of desire within a benevolent patriarchy.

The terms of economic equilibrium are stated baldly by the opening montage of images which serves to illustrate the message on the soundtrack: 'You cannot get something for nothing.' The film sets out to prove the 'truth' of this dictum through the attempt by a group of employees to rob the department store where they work. They are employed by Jerome Morris, whose policy it is to give jobs to ex-convicts, countering his wife's belief that criminals cannot be changed because they are 'born that way'. The department store is the positive alternative to prison, a place of learning rather than simple incarceration. Prison is where criminals are punished for transgression of the Law (LS). In Morris' store, when the criminals' break-in is interrupted by Morris and Helen, he leaves her to demonstrate economically and morally that crime does not pay. His role as benevolent patriarch is underlined by the reducing of the criminals to the status of children. Helen delivers her (Brechtian) lecture in the toy department, using a blackboard, while they listen, seated in kiddy cars, clutching toys. Thus this Law (PS/LS) is distinguished from its institutionalised counterpart (LS), in an assertion of the economic status quo as that which is learned as 'good sense', rather than simply enforced, as it is by the Law (LS).

But the film's project is crucially twofold — not only to demonstrate the truth of the message of the opening montage sequence, but also to resolve the problem of the romance between Helen and Joe. This is rendered problematic by the taboo placed by the Law (LS) against marriages between paroled convicts. However, Helen, seeking to hide

94

her criminal past from Joe, tells him that they must keep their marriage a secret because Morris has placed a ban on marriages between store employees. The Law (PS) as represented by Morris is thus rendered benevolent when compared to the Law (LS) represented by Dayton, the parole officer, in that Helen asserts an imaginary ban by Morris precisely in order that it can subsequently be proved untrue. It is thus emphasised that Morris is *not* the oppressive face of the Law (PS distinguished from LS).

Joe's desire for Helen is dependent upon her retaining a certain idealised status. He must believe her when she tells him that there was no other man, and that she will never lie to him. This status is to a large extent based on the denial of Helen's desire, outside its role in aiding the definition of Joe's place within the Law (PS/LS). When they visit a dance hall a close-up of Helen's face, gazing out of frame, is followed by a close-up of Joe *not* looking at her, while on the soundtrack the words of a song speak of the 'kind of man girls dream about'. In other words Helen's gaze expresses a female desire which only seeks its object, and cannot enter into a reciprocal relationship with it. The voice of that desire is present only as repressed and displaced — the soundtrack divorced from the image track. In fact, the text works to deny the idea of the female as such. Joe's desire for Helen is initially marked by his lack of knowledge as to her status. He rejects the sexual advances of a woman in the store who displays her leg to him, a moment balanced by the shot of Joe and Helen's hands touching as they pass on the escalator. But this is not innocence as romance, rather innocence as confusion. They are seen before a shop window, with Helen remarking that a perfume ('Hour of Ecstasy') does something for 'a girl's soul'. When she asks Joe if he sees it, he replies 'No'. His response is to ask her if she would like to be a man, to which she answers, 'No . . . yes . . . I don't know', and finally that she thinks it might be simpler. Joe claims that he has not thought much of women before, and that he told Helen about his criminal record because 'I would never have believed a fella and a girl could be friends like us'. He is attracted to her precisely because she represents the possibility of the pre-Oedipal fantasy of a 'girl' who is like a 'fella'. The status of their romance/relationship as a fantasy of which they become projections is pointed to by the shot of dancing neon figures on a sign, which dissolves into a shot of Joe and Helen dancing. A little later they are seen through a curtain, framed by the embroidered pattern of two white dancing figures.

But Helen's agreeing to marry Joe means that he learns the truth; the ambiguity about her is resolved. The problem posed is that Joe, now aware of the status of the female body, cannot as a result identify with the father figure. Through the displacement effected by Helen's fiction, Morris, the benevolent patriarch, has become identified with the threatening face of the Law (LS), for which Joe attaining the object of his desire is a punishable transgression. Joe first tries to avoid the dilemma by a return to the plane of fantasy. He pretends not to know Helen's name in front of Nellie, and also substitutes a tour of restaurants for a trip-around-the-world honeymoon. But the real threat of the father intrudes, by way of a joke. Joe's response to his Chinese fortune cookie, which contains the message that he will have ten sons, is 'Let's get out of here'.

Because the Law (ps) intrudes but is denied, Helen's status remains problematic. Joe learns that she has lied to him, that she has a criminal past, at the ex-convicts' Christmas Eve dinner, where they fantasise about their past life in prison, without women. But this fantasy of a return to an all-male world is ultimately as impossible as Joe's fantasy of living outside the Law (ps). The denial of the female body disturbs the body of the text. The scene is marked by disruption of both image and soundtrack (visual distortion, loud chanting), and the attempt at the illusory return of the flashback. But Joe cannot accept the unidealised form of Helen. His fears about her being unfaithful are displaced on to the knowledge that she has spent time in prison; i.e. the same Law (ls) which holds him, and whose hold is signified by his parole card, demonstrates its hold over her by the same sign. The taboo against them marrying has earlier been signified by close-ups, from each of their points of view, of their parole cards. Joe must acknowledge that the enigma of the female is only solvable within the terms of the Law (ps). And it is Morris, the benevolent father, who offers the image of Helen which solves the problem in those terms. The image of the mother is substituted for that of 'the plaster saint' (as she is described by the ex-convicts).

The fantasy of Helen as mother is realised in two distinct ways, as though to separate the role of the mother as function of the Law (ps) from her role in 'human relations'. The symbolic mother, teaching the children/criminals the error of their ways, on Morris' behalf, is distinguished from the 'real' mother (bearer of Joe's child) in order that Joe can be seen to reject the former and accept the latter. But the fact that he still only attains Helen within the terms of the Law (ps and ls) is emphasised by the scene which shows him obtaining the 'Hour of Ecstasy' perfume. The perfume previously signified his ignorance about the status of the female, an ignorance which has been corrected. But when he is pointedly shown paying for the perfume, as opposed to stealing it, then the significance of his acquisition of knowledge is made clear. His Oedipal journey is inextricably bound up with the mainte- nance of the economic order of things. The final shot is a close-up of Joe and Helen's baby, held by Gimpey, one of the ex-convicts. On to him has been displaced (jokingly) the idea of male/female confusion, the sign of disequilibrium. Gimpey has found the missing Helen in the hospital — by imagining what he would do if he were a pregnant girl.

96

A lesson . . .

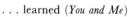

. . . learned (*You and Me*)

The most immediately obvious common factor uniting *You Only Live Once* and *You and Me* is that they are both rather strange versions of 1930s problem pictures, in that they both deal with problems faced by ex-convicts. The Law (LS) is, as a direct result, unavoidably invoked when discussing the films, in whatever context. This invocation can be read as a kind of convenient cover for the investigation of the female which proceeds at the core of the narrative in each case, the problem for the Law (PS). Most criticism of course ignores this core; the films are problematic problem pictures because they deal with 'Fate' rather than confront social issues head-on. There is also the Romantic option of the 'doomed couple' as a strategy for placing *You Only Live Once*. But, almost paradoxically, when the Law (LS) is largely repressed from a subsequent text, in this case *Scarlet Street*, then the investigative core of the previous films becomes all the more apparent, present here in a purer form, or rather with a different cover.

The opening scene of *Scarlet Street* succinctly establishes the terms of the narrative to follow. Chris Cross, a middle-aged cashier, is presented with a watch, for long service, by his boss Hogarth. The celebrations are interrupted by the arrival of a woman in a car, with whom Hogarth leaves. Chris confides to his friend Charlie that he wonders 'what it's like to be loved by a young girl like that'. However, the simple Oedipal triangle is already marked by a heavy emphasis on the link between desire and the subject/gaze/'fixed' object axis. Woman is constituted as the anonymous object of the gaze, that of the characters within the text and that of the spectator, with the two being distinguished. The men at the party rush to the window, and one of them cries, 'Get a load of that dame'. There is then a cut to a medium close-up of the woman in the car, a shot from the spectator's privileged point of view. The woman awakens in Chris the desire to gaze. But also the possibility of being gazed at/desired, a wish marked as a regression: 'You know, nobody ever looked at me like that [as the woman looks at Hogarth] . . . not even when I was young.' What is subsequently traced in *Scarlet Street* is the trajectory of Chris' desire, in terms of the wish to fix the image of the woman (in his case through the medium of painting), a desire which causes his descent into madness, because in fulfilling it he does not simply assert his subjectivity but, on the contrary, loses it in the castrated female body which he constitutes not simply as object but as a reflection of himself. That which looks back . . .

The introduction of Kitty and Johnny, her pimp, takes place specifically in terms of Chris' gaze and, by implication, as an answer to the earlier question, 'I wonder what it's like . . .'. A shot of Chris looking out of frame is followed by a shot, from his point of view, of the two of them fighting. After he has knocked down Johnny, Chris is seen covering, and then slowly uncovering, his eyes. In the bar to which Kitty takes him she asks him why he's looking at her, as he watches her looking

Objectified/emasculated beneath the portrait's gaze (*Scarlet Street*)

out of the window and gazing at herself in a hand-mirror. Chris claims to be a 'full-time' painter, and when Kitty asks him what work he thinks she does, he replies that she is an actress, i.e. he fantasises her as a woman without 'identity', a pure object of the gaze. But his fantasy is qualified. He is constituted as the object of her gaze, as she looks down at him while denying him entry to her home, and his fears of a kind of Oedipal transgression are marked. When he claims to be 'old enough to be your father', she replies that he is 'not so old'; and as he asks, 'Who's Johnny?', he is objectified in a shot looking down the steps at him below.

The threat posed by the absent figure of Johnny is mirrored in Chris' home by the portrait of his wife Adele's first husband, Homer Higgins, missing believed dead. Beneath the gaze which emanates from the portrait Chris is objectified and effectively emasculated, often seen wearing an apron and performing the domestic tasks his wife refuses. Chris' unsuccessful adoption of Homer's place in the symbolic order of the family is now replaced by the possibility of the assumption of subjectivity via his fantasy centred on Kitty. She has given him a flower ('So you won't forget me'), a pure fetish object which Chris is seen painting. The significance of the painting as the product of Chris' subjective vision, in the 'concrete' sense of the gaze, is indicated in the comment made by his friend Charlie's voice-over: 'You mean you see this . . . when you look at that', as the camera pans from the painting to the flower. Adele then fills the space which separates Chris from the desired object of his gaze. As he starts to articulate his fantasy ('You see, when I look at that flower') the door opens and Adele appears, 'framed' between Chris/Charlie and the picture.

The regressive status of Chris' desire is suggested by Johnny, as he reads the letter Chris has written to Kitty. He describes it as sounding 'like a schoolboy trying to make a date. You must be robbing the cradle'. This is taken up when Chris, at the café with Kitty, impersonates the robin's whistle he learned as a child, and tells her that 'I feel like a kid myself today'. But Chris' return to 'innocence' goes hand in hand with his description of himself as a repressed individual, a person who keeps things 'bottled up'. And what is 'bottled up' is made clear when Adele, after complaining that he paints girls and snakes, suggests that he will soon be painting women without clothes, to which Chris replies: 'I never saw a woman without any clothes.' Chris compares a painting to a love affair, but what becomes apparent is that his desire for Kitty, which is inextricably bound up with his wish to paint her, centres on the possibility of a disavowal of the castrated status of the female body — a return to the 'innocence' of pre-Oedipal notions of bisexuality. Chris' place within the patriarchal order is confused and unresolved. He has taken the place of the absent father, the ex-policeman, representative of the Law (LS/PS), but remains trapped beneath the latter's emasculating gaze (Homer's picture). The stereotyped roles of Adele as bullying harridan and Chris as aproned, harassed husband signify Chris' confusion over what is signified by male/female, a confusion he tries to resolve through his fantasy of Kitty. In order for his idyll with her to succeed the Law (PS) must be repressed. So he tells her, after he has established her in the apartment, that he does not want her to borrow money from Johnny. His fears emerge crudely in the painting which shows a woman standing beneath a beam of light from a lamp, with the word 'Loans' above a window in the background, and a snake, with its threatening tongue extended towards the woman.

The narrative now works to fulfil Chris' fantasy concerning the uncastrated woman. This is achieved through the conspiracy, worked by Johnny and Kitty, to pass off Chris' paintings as having been painted by her. The result is confusion over the sexual identity of the artist. The artist whom Johnny meets in the street selling paintings claims, 'I never would have guessed it was a woman'; and Janeway, the art critic, says that he can usually tell whether a canvas is by a man or a woman, but 'You fooled me completely, Miss Marsh'. He describes her work as having 'a masculine force'. In addition Kitty repeats, word for word, remarks previously made by Chris about art. The importance of the paintings as regards the status which Chris attaches to Kitty's body is stressed as wordplay. Kitty says that she will allow Chris to paint her: he kneels and accepts the proffered foot, whose toenails he will paint.

100

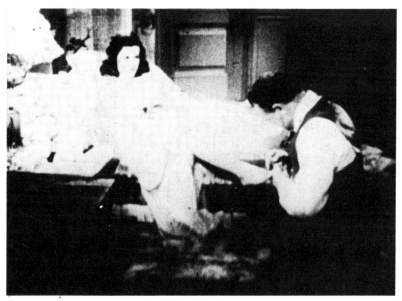

Painting a body (*Scarlet Street*)

When Adele sees Chris' paintings in the window of Dellarowe's gallery, signed with Kitty's name, the switch begins. She accuses Chris of copying Kitty's work. He initially responds to this discovery in terms of the loss of his sexuality, the threat of castration. A dismembering close-up shows the kitchen knife which Chris has dropped stuck in the floor between his feet. It is as though his masculine subjectivity were further threatened by Kitty's appropriation of his work as hers. But subsequently Chris turns this threat on its head, interpreting her action as the realisation of his fantasy. She has not taken his work, rather he has taken her name. Her deception enables him to enter into a narcissistic identification with the uncastrated woman, the woman whose work has 'masculine force'. As he puts it: 'Why, it's just like a dream . . . Why, it's just like we were married, only I take your name.' And it is at this point of total narcissism that he finally constitutes her as image, claiming 'Well, that gives me a little authority around here'. He seats her on the podium and shines the spotlight on her, with the words 'Know what we're gonna call this? Self-portrait'.

But Chris' triumph is short-lived, as the Law (PS) is reasserted through its several faces (Homer, Johnny, Hogarth). The fantasy actually carries over into Chris' denial of the memory of Homer's emasculating gaze. Homer returns from the dead but becomes a function of Chris' new-found power. The strength of his gaze is reduced (he now sports an eye-patch) and he is lured back to Adele by the signalling light

101

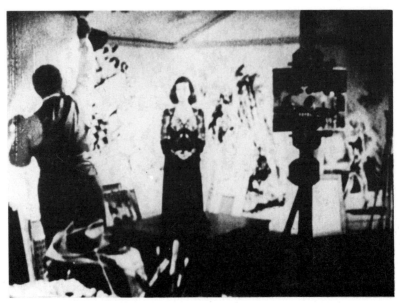

Self-portrait (*Scarlet Street*)

of Chris' torch. This is after he has stepped from the darkness into the pool of light cast by a street lamp, like the woman in Chris' painting. At this point, however, the fantasy begins to crumble. Chris returns to Kitty but finds her with Johnny. The couple are shown embracing, as the object of Chris' gaze. As in an earlier scene the record they are playing is stuck, this time endlessly repeating the words 'in love . . . in love . . . in love . . .' This 'disturbance' on the soundtrack also refers back to the scene where Chris steals Adele's bonds, which was preceded by interference on the radio during 'The Happy Household Hour'. This in turn was linked with Chris gazing at the portrait of Homer gazing back at him. This new aural disturbance therefore flashes back to the site of the previous symbolic order in which Chris' place was uncertain, and from which he believed he had escaped. But no escape is possible. Chris' narcissistic identification with Kitty is destroyed by Johnny's intrusion, the reminder of the symbolic order.

Chris' loss of subjectivity is total. When he returns to Kitty, to forgive her, she fatally mistakes him for Johnny (in fact Johnny had earlier told Janeway that *he* was Chris), a confusion echoed on the soundtrack as Chris mistakes Kitty's laughter for crying. And having punished Kitty for her transgression of his fantasy, and destroyed his now false reflection, Chris is denied even this assertion of self—Johnny is arrested, tried and executed for the murder Chris committed. The usual distinction is now drawn between the two systems of the Law (ps/ls) .

102

Johnny is wrongly convicted by the legal system, while the narrative contrives to present the patriarch in a benevolent light. Hogarth, the trigger for Chris' fantasy, does not have him arrested for stealing from the firm and thus dissociates himself from the Law (LS), a similar tactic to Whitney's in *You Only Live Once*. But he also tells Chris he knows that 'It was a woman, wasn't it?'.

Chris, having denied his subjectivity during the murder trial by telling the court that he cannot paint, is now punished by being thrust into a world where he is the marked object of the privileged gaze of the camera/spectator, a savagely ironic reminder of his narcissistic desire to be looked at by his reflection. His loss of subjectivity is also signified by both image and soundtrack being 'out of control'. He is shown in a hotel room conversing with the whispering voices of Kitty and Johnny which he can hear, while the neon sign outside punctuates the darkness with flashes of light. And at the end of the film other figures in the street are dissolved from the image, leaving Chris as the sole object of the camera/spectator gaze. There is one final ironic reference to his fantasy. As he passes Dellarowe's gallery Kitty's portrait, painted by him, is carried out. The picture frame fills the film frame, the image looks at Chris who looks back at it, as he did with Homer's portrait. A comment by someone in the shop — 'her masterpiece' — is followed by a cut to Chris, now the object not only of the camera/spectator gaze, but also of the gaze of the image which was supposed to be the very expression of his subjectivity.

Image out of control (*Scarlet Street*)

103

What *Scarlet Street* makes absolutely clear, through its discourse on 'art', is that woman has significance only as the object (the Other) to be investigated, in relation to which the masculine subject defines his place within the Law (ps). Kitty's image fixed within the picture frame within the film frame is like a logical end point, an underlining. It is interesting, then, to look at a film like *Secret Beyond the Door,* which seems at first glance to counterbalance this tendency. It introduces a female voice as discourse, in the form of Celia's voice-over which accompanies much of the depicted action. Similarly the image track in the first section of the film consists largely of the visual realisation of her memories, in the form of flashback. The main body of the narrative then consists of *her* investigation of Mark Lamphere, her attempts to open the door of room number 7 and discover its secret, which is the secret of Mark's troubled mind. The final equilibrium, here a shot showing Celia lying with Mark's head in her lap, is ostensibly the result of her achieving her desire. She has solved the problem of Mark's repressed childhood memory, whereby he believed that his mother had locked him in his room, from where he had seen her driving away with 'another man'. In fact, this pat 'Freudian' resolution can be read as an almost arbitrary strategy adopted by the text to conclude *its* investigation of Celia, to fix her place within the terms of its order. Any notion of the possibility of female discourse within the text is always undercut, (dis)placed, qualified.

This is apparent in the opening scene in the church. Celia's voice-over dominates but is 'troubled': 'This is no time to think of danger, this is my wedding day.' Desire and danger are immediately linked. Her voice-over then describes the church, while an accompanying camera movement illustrates her words. But are the words hers?. She says, 'Mark says it's a felicitous structure', and then quotes what is presumably his description. And the camera movement ends on the image of Mark standing with his back to the camera's gaze; in other words, she is denied the object of her look. Similarly her flashback illustrates at first only her reliance on Rick, her brother, who describes himself as 'mother, father and cheque signer' for her. The possibility of desire she associates only with the potential loss of this ungendered being. Her embracing Rick is interrupted by the arrival of Bob, described as a 'thoroughly eligible young man'. But as she shakes hands with him the camera pans across to Rick, while her voice-over is heard saying, 'When you died, Rick, I was lonely'.

The second stage of the flashback (her holiday in Mexico) contrives to constitute Celia as the object which her own discourse cannot know. *She* is the mystery to be solved. Her voice-over links the threat of violence (the knife thrown by one of the combatants in a fight, which lands by her hand) with the feeling of being scrutinised, of being the object of another's gaze: 'I felt eyes touching me like fingers.' There is then a shot

'A man I don't know at all' (*Secret Beyond the Door*)

of Mark looking. Moreover she mystifies the power of his gaze: the image of her it produces is more 'real' than her image within her own flashback. She claims that 'he saw behind my make-up what no one had ever seen. Something I didn't know was there'. He is posited as the source of knowledge, possessor of the truth, telling her: 'You're not a bit like you. You aren't what you seem to be.' He is shown back to camera, relaying the position of the spectator, while she is transfixed by his gaze. As the narrative returns to the wedding a shot from her point of view of the priest pans across to Mark, who walks towards her/the camera/ spectator but into shadow. Meanwhile her voice-over reiterates her lack of knowledge concerning him: 'I'm marrying a stranger, a man I don't know at all.' A double mystery is thus established, but on unequal terms. Celia 'knows' (sees) neither herself nor Mark, while Mark 'knows' (sees through) her, and will eventually know himself through her.

When Mark leaves her on the honeymoon (after finding himself locked out of her room) his absence does not primarily signify the mystery surrounding him, but rather the awakening of Celia's fears of abandonment. She is left only with the image of herself that she does not understand, as she is seen watching herself in a mirror. Her voice-over questions his behaviour ('Why had he gone?') in terms of her loss ('Why doesn't he love me any more?'). Mark's absence when she arrives at his old family home, Levender Falls, then causes her to doubt the truth of what is the object of her own gaze. As she and Carrie, Mark's sister,

105

arrive at the house there is a cut to a shot of a window, from which a woman is looking. This is followed by a shot from the window of Celia and Carrie getting out of the car. There is then a shot from Celia's point of view of the window, from which the woman draws back. But Carrie tells Celia that the person she saw was probably Mark's son, David. The revelation of Mark's status as father, coupled with the confusion over the sexual identity of the figure at the window, flashes back to the scene with Rick, simultaneously mother and father for Celia, and the figure who could not be replaced.

Celia's dilemma is to be caught between two roles, both of which she is denied. Her status as wife is threatened by the memory of Eleanor, Mark's previous wife. When she claims that it would be foolish to be jealous she is seen before a mirror, the classic image of self-deception. And when she later tells David that 'I'll never try to take your mother's place', he replies that she could not. Her place is mirrored grotesquely by the figure of Miss Robey, the image of woman 'made strange', marked by a wound, signified by the scarf with which she covers the supposedly scarred half of her face. Carrie claims that she uses this disfigurement as a hold over Mark. In other words Celia's place is that of the pure signifier of difference, that by which Mark will come to know himself. After Mark arrives and is disturbed by the flowers (lilacs) worn by Celia in her lapel (a further reminder of childhood trauma), she is seen driving, while her voice-over proclaims her desire to return to Rick, the father/mother, the fantasy of the cancellation of sexual difference. But Rick is also the representative of the patriarchal economic order ('cheque signer'), and therefore, as Celia admits, would send her back: 'I conjured him up and he read me the riot act.'

What subsequently occurs is the gradual denial of Celia's discourse, and the assertion of Mark's, of which she becomes a function. This is apparent in the scene where visitors to the house are shown Mark's 'collection' of re-creations of rooms in which murders have been committed. Celia's voice-over is now replaced by Mark's. For example, she looks out of frame and there is a cut to the chair in which, as described by Mark's voice-over, an old lady was tied up and murdered. Her look becomes the means of illustrating the male voice-over. What she does not know about Mark is emphasised precisely by what she does not see. Her words to Bob ('I know Mark — he wouldn't do anything unfair') are followed by laughter on the soundtrack and a shot of an empty doorway, which is held while voices discuss Mark, his two wives' money, etc. The camera then pulls back to reveal Celia and Bob gazing at the empty doorway.

Celia's discovery of the secret of room number 7, her realisation that it is a murder room 'waiting for me', is provoked by her desire to save Mark, and to resolve the split between Mark and David. A shot from her point of view of Mark carrying an injured dog is a heavily ironic

Woman 'made strange' (*Secret Beyond the Door*)

projection of her fantasy concerning the 'truth' about Mark, the inner
goodness waiting to be revealed. Her investigation and discovery
prolongs the irony. While obtaining the key to the room she encounters
Miss Robey with her face uncovered, and revealed as unscarred. The
suggestion of the woman as uncastrated is jokily picked up by the phallic
imagery (keys and candles) associated with Celia's assertion of self, her
determination to know. Power is suggested, as usual with Lang, by the
beam of light from her torch with which she illuminates the lock, and
which is then matched by the shot of the room seen from her point of
view. But when she sees the trimmed candle she realises that her
discovery means her death. She is the next intended murder victim.
Consequently she is now 'removed' from the text. She runs through the
darkness, with no light, and then out into the fog, where she sees Mark
approaching her. She screams and the image goes black . . .

Her discourse is now definitively replaced by Mark's, as is made clear
by the 'imaginary' trial in which he questions himself, constituting
himself as subject and object of that discourse. What disturbs him, what
causes him to think the way he does, is, needless to say, the domination of
his life by women. Celia then appears in the doorway, framed as the
object of a shot from his point of view. As she walks towards him the
angle is reversed but, significantly, the shot is not *exactly* from her point of
view. The possibility of equilibrium is suggested by a cut to a shot
framing them both, as she tells him that she loves him. But Mark's

Secret Beyond the Door: self-questioning

voice-over continues to posit *her* as problem: he can't be alone with her, he must get as far away from her as possible. True equilibrium only returns when Celia submits to Mark's fantasy, and enters the (now burning) room which has been prepared for her death. Celia's ultimate negation of herself as subject ('I'd rather be dead than live without you') is matched by equilibrium: a shot of Mark in the doorway seen from Celia's point of view is followed by a shot of her seen from his. At this point the repressed memory can be released since the narrative has worked through Mark's fantasy wish to kill his mother, through the utter denial of subjectivity, to the point of death, on the part of Celia. Woman's 'place' is firmly defined and equilibrium restored as Mark carries her from the house. This equilibrium is noticeably dependent on displacement. Just as Celia reveals to Mark that it was Carrie, and not his mother, who locked him in his room when he was a child, so, in the present, the now 'unproblematic' figure of Celia is offset by the disturbed behaviour of Miss Robey. The fact that it was she who started the fire, not realising that Mark was in the house, clearly marks her as the threat to stability, as opposed to Celia who is the means by which it is attained. Miss Robey also makes clear the significance of this stability, since it was she who rendered illusory the wound which was the basis of her relationship with Mark. Equilibrium demands that such a presence should now be removed . . .

108

Both *Scarlet Street* and *Secret Beyond the Door* can be seen as dramatisations of the actual idea of discourse, the assertion of subject over object — meaning always, crudely, male over female. In *Scarlet Street* the dramatisation takes the form of painting, in *Secret Beyond the Door* it is a battle of voice(over)s. The fact that the 'heroes' of several of Lang's later films are overt producers of discourse, whether journalist, writer or news reporter, is clearly of interest in this respect. The investigation of the female continues but is no longer the 'natural' work of the narrative rendered as sourceless. The position of the anonymous, invisible subject of the meta-discourse of the film as a whole (the name Lang) is, to a degree, mirrored by these figures. To a degree. For example, the 'reflections' are split and dispersed by the co-presence of the previously mentioned newspaper owners. Nevertheless the film work is denaturalised, the investigative core which runs through the Lang-text is exposed. *The Blue Gardenia* is a useful example of this process.

In the opening minutes of the film two characters are seen 'mirrored' by their own images. As journalist Casey Mayo walks towards the lift in the West Coast Telephone Company building he is shown in the same shot as an image of himself, advertising his contributions to the *Chronicle* newspaper. There is then a dissolve to the face of Crystal, a worker in the company, who is being sketched by artist Harry Prebble. Prebble is interrupted by a somewhat hysterical phone call from a woman, Rose, after which he is seen gazing at the sketch he has made. The two images within the filmic image clearly signify very different things. The picture of Casey is linked with the idea of the reporter as originating subject of a discourse, a text which describes and circumscribes an object. The drawing of Crystal signifies the opposite, constituting her as precisely the object of such a discourse, this time that of the artist. The drawing which renders the woman as fixed, controlled object of the male gaze is contrasted with the hysterical, disturbing female voice, the threat posed by the woman not fixed as image, unseen at that point by Prebble.

Prebble gazing at the sketch is followed by a dissolve to a shot of Norah, work/flatmate of Crystal, posing in an evening dress, the object of the privileged gaze of the spectator. A third image within the image is introduced — a photograph of Norah's boyfriend, serving in Korea. What this image signifies is precisely Norah's inability to recognise and circumscribe reality, and her consequent flight into fantasy. Because she cannot share a birthday meal with him she will share it with his photograph. In other words she attempts to treat the image as the absent object in the 'reality' which it reflects. The photograph becomes the object of her discourse as she toasts it with the words 'Hullo darling'. What destroys her fetishistic fantasy is the addition of sound to the image. As she reads a letter from him its words are spoken by the voice-over of the absent lover, telling her that he has fallen in love with a nurse.

Subject of a discourse: image doubled (*The Blue Gardenia*)

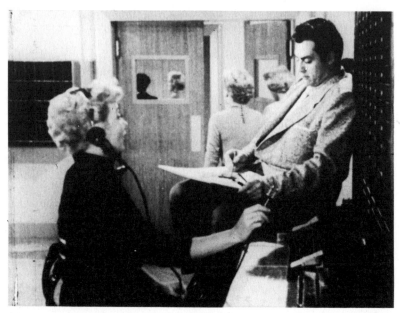

Object of a discourse (*The Blue Gardenia*)

Flight into fantasy (*The Blue Gardenia*)

As Norah is made the object of the discourse of the voice-over (the 'you' spoken by the 'I'), so she renounces her subjectivity by accepting Prebble's invitation to dinner, which he believed he was addressing to Crystal. At the restaurant Norah expresses her desire to repress the memory of the earlier part of the evening, a desire which mirrors the repression by Prebble (and, in terms of the subsequent 'murder mystery', by the filmic discourse itself) of the memory of the demands made by Rose. It also points forward to Norah's later 'inability' to remember the time spent with Prebble. Norah now becomes the reflection of an image, as was Crystal. The picture in Prebble's flat which he tells Norah he must finish that night shows a man and a woman in front of a mirror, mirroring the moment of crisis to come. When Norah falls asleep on the couch, Prebble is shown looking out of frame at her, while on the wall behind him is a picture of a female figure. What provokes the struggle in front of the mirror is the return of Norah's sense of subjectivity, initially signified by her confusing Prebble with the memory of her soldier boyfriend. At this point the gap in the text is established (marked by the visual distortion which renders the image unreadable, the sign of Norah losing consciousness) which it will be the work of Casey Mayo, as the 'voice of truth', to fill.

Norah claims of the evening that 'There's nothing I can remember'. But what is being repressed is revealed to be the breaking of the mirror,

111

the destruction of her reflected image. This is heavily signalled. A shot of Norah examining herself in the mirror the next morning is followed by a shot of the shattered mirror in Prebble's apartment, where the police are attempting to reconstruct the murder. Similarly, when a girl at the telephone exchange drops a handmirror, a shot, from Norah's point of view, of the broken glass is followed by an inserted image of Prebble's mirror breaking. What is at stake is as much the reconstruction of her image as the crime. This is made clear by Casey's conversation with a blind flower-seller at the Blue Gardenia Club. She tells him about Norah's perfume, her voice, the material her dress was made of, but obviously can offer no clue as regards what she looked like, her image.

Norah can gain access to the truth, regain her subjectivity, fill the gap, only through the male discourse of the Law (L S/ P S) of which she is made the marked object. As usual the two systems of the Law are distinguished, and it is the patriarchal system, through the intervention of Casey, which enables Norah to 'know herself' again. The legal system is once more posited as both threatening and mistaken with regard to Norah. The threat is embodied in the use of light to suggest the gaze which, in taking Norah as its object, would 'capture' her. The lightning flashes which accompanied the moment of crisis are picked up by the beam of the police car headlights in which Norah is caught when burning the dress in the incinerator, and also by the photographers' flashbulbs from which she shields her eyes after having her fingerprints taken. It is specifically the *look* of the Law (L S) which she seeks to avoid. For example, at one point a police car pulls up at some petrol pumps, a few yards from where Norah is telephoning Casey. A shot of the car drawing up is retrospectively suggested to be from Norah's point of view by the shot of her looking out of frame which follows. Another shot of the car shows a policeman looking out of frame to where Norah's look implied she was. But the next shot shows the phone booth, now empty.

Light and the gaze 'come together' definitively, in terms of Norah as the object of the male gaze, when she presents herself to Casey in the darkened newspaper offices. She is seen at the end of the office, the object of a shot from his point of view, with the *Chronicle* sign flashing on and off above her head. This shot is the culmination of a process whereby Norah's sense of self becomes dependent on her acknowledgment of Casey as the voice of truth, with 'truth' signified by the discourse of the newspaper. The newspaper in fact becomes the means whereby Casey fulfils his ambiguous wish, expressed as 'I want to be the guy to nail her . . . my girlfriend, the Blue Gardenia'. Thus a shot, from Norah's point of view, of a newspaper headline referring to the murder is followed by a shot of her reading, with the previously mentioned photograph of Casey occupying the left of the frame. The process becomes very overt with his 'Letter to an Unknown Murderess', which is printed in the *Chronicle*. A series of shots shows various people reading the letter, while

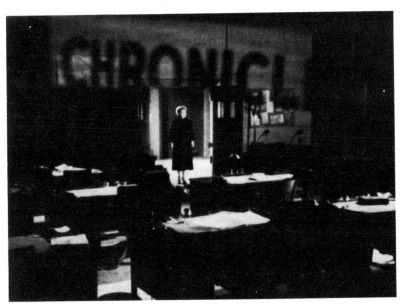

The Blue Gardenia: Norah 'nailed'

Casey's voice-over doubles the printed words. The final shot of the series shows Norah, the object of the gaze of the camera/spectator, but also, by virtue of the 'first person' voice-over ('There's nowhere to run . . . except to me'), the object of what could be read as a subjective shot with the camera gaze identified with that of Casey.

What happens when Norah becomes the direct object of his gaze is that Casey is faced with the dilemma of having to reconcile her as object of his desire with the fact that she comes to him as woman as potential threat, that is a murderess. The dilemma has emerged earlier with the lighthearted reference to 'My girlfriend . . . the Blue Gardenia', but this tone was only possible while 'contact' was mediated through the discourse of the newspaper. When the female image becomes the direct object of Casey's unmediated gaze, the dilemma is initially displaced through the idea of woman as 'mystery'. This is marked metaphorically when Norah escapes from the bar where she is talking to Casey and disappears into the fog. Casey tells Sleepy, his photographer partner, that she is the wrong type for his 'little black book' (woman reduced to unproblematic object of desire) and that he doesn't meet 'girls like that' very often. The nature of the mystery surrounding Norah is such that it can only be 'solved' by a further process of displacement. This first takes the form of the introduction of an imaginary third person — the 'friend' on whose behalf Norah claims to be acting, who 'wants to remember, but just can't'. The imaginary is then gradually transformed into the real.

Offered to the male gaze (*The Blue Gardenia*)

When Casey sees Crystal in the bar, he attempts to fix her as the murderess but is thwarted by the revelation that Norah is in the next booth. The final stage in the displacement is achieved through the musical 'clue' which sends Casey to Rose Miller.

The return of the woman 'repressed' from the narrative enables the similarly repressed moment of crisis to be resolved. The breaking of Prebble's mirror is mirrored by the glass from the broken mirror with which Rose attempts to commit suicide. As Norah sees herself mirrored in the scarred form of Rose, another woman as bearer of the wound, an equilibrium is restored. Norah looking at, seeing herself in, Rose is intercut with shots of Casey looking at Norah, now the unproblematic, because rendered unmysterious, object of his gaze. Norah's subsequent rejection of Casey's advances, her final assertion of self, is marked as ironic, a postponement of the inevitable form of equilibrium. It immediately follows the moment when Norah, Crystal and the third flatmate, Sally, offer themselves to the 'look' of the reporters' cameras. For Norah, the filling of the gap in the text means that the threat of the male gaze is removed, and she no longer shields her eyes from the light of the flashbulbs. But this stresses her status as *object* of the gaze/desire. The gap was caused precisely by her attempt to assert herself as subject of desire, to make the objects of that desire interchangeable (her soldier boyfriend for Prebble) in the way that she offered herself to Prebble as substitute object for Crystal. The equilibrium restored is that of the

114

male/subject female/object relation which was established at the film's beginning.

A review of *The Blue Gardenia* in the *Monthly Film Bulletin* correctly noted that 'the real killer is so obtrusively planted, that one has few doubts about the outcome'. The fact that the spectator is privileged with the knowledge that the text is repressing the previously introduced figure of Rose Miller means that the process traced by the narrative is as much to do with specularity and subject/object relations as with 'whodunit'. The climax of the text is the capture of Norah, constituted as the object of a shot from the point of view of Casey/the spectator/the camera/Lang, rather than the revelation — no revelation at all — of Rose's guilt.

This opposition between the ostensible 'point' of the narrative being the filling of a gap in the spectator's knowledge, and the narrative constituting a representation of a specular process, is taken to extremes in *Beyond a Reasonable Doubt*. The gap to be filled here is the knowledge that Tom Garrett is actually guilty of the murder for which, in an attempt to prove that circumstantial evidence can be used to convict an innocent man, he is deliberately 'framing' himself. At the beginning of the film Austin Spencer, publisher and father of Susan, Tom's fiancé, instigates their plan with these words: 'A fictitious story wouldn't prove anything: it could only be proven by a fact that no one could deny.' But the subsequent revelation of Tom's guilt means that the intervening narrative proves nothing. It only depicts, excessively in a fictitious story, the clues which betoken that guilt. The ostensible challenge from Spencer to Thompson, the District Attorney, is an empty one. Thompson describes his position simply: 'I'm here to uphold the laws of this state.' And it is the Law (LS/PS) which the film 'upholds'. The text does not progress but is circular. It begins with a shot of a prisoner being led to the electric chair, and ends with a shot of Garrett being led back to his cell, prior to his execution. It should perhaps be stressed that there is no investigation of any psychological resonance with regard to Garrett's position or character, nothing resembling 'transfer of guilt' for example. What is shown is an inevitable process of which the characters are pure functions.

At an early stage of their plan Garrett and Spencer decide to exclude Susan from the secret. The process of ensnaring Garrett causes the relationship between him and Susan to break down. This is made clear when Garrett receives a phone call which, in retrospect, the spectator can assume is from Patti Grey, the dancer he murders. The person Garrett is speaking to is not shown, and the scene ends with a shot of him merely looking worried. There is then a dissolve to a close-up of a cigarette lighter inscribed 'To Tom From Susan'. Garrett tells Susan that the phone call was from his publisher, and that they will have to

Beyond a Reasonable Doubt: Susan in her father's place

postpone their marriage because of the pressure of his work. Garrett's book ('fiction') is then replaced by Spencer's plan ('fact') but the result is the same. The threat posed to the relationship by the plan is discussed by the two men as they are driving to the murder spot to arrange more 'evidence', and when Garrett's trial is shown on television it is Susan's watching and reaction which is stressed. When she visits Garrett in prison, the physical/visual separation effected by the bars and metal lattice is doubled on the soundtrack by her doubts about his claim that the pictures taken of the 'evidence' will prove his innocence: 'I don't know what to believe now.' There is a crucial dissolve from Garrett in the death cell to Susan at her dead father's desk, declaring 'I am this newspaper now' and instructing the newspapermen to help Garrett's case. In fact, her assumption of her father's role means that, ironically, the process which he instigated is carried through. The journalists' investigations uncover the name Emma. It is the uttering of this word by Garrett which betrays his guilt to Susan, and ensures his death. Spencer, as the representative of the Law (PS), the prospective 'father-in-law', sets out to destroy Garrett. As he remarks to his prospective victim, 'If we're lucky you'd get the chair'. Garrett is denied the object of his desire, Susan, by the plan which ensures his punishment for his transgression of the Law (LS), the murder of Patti Grey. Once again the two systems signified by 'the Law' are seen to be inextricably linked, and their goals coincide.

116

The death of Spencer at the point when he is about to prove Tom's innocence simply enables this link to be made explicit. Both Spencer and Garrett, the men in Susan's life, are replaced by the 'lawman', Lieutenant Kennedy, a former boyfriend of hers. It is Kennedy to whom Susan betrays Garrett's guilt, significantly in terms of the denial of desire: 'The man I saw in prison wasn't the man I loved — he was a stranger, someone I never knew.' This implicit replacement of Garrett by Kennedy is then balanced by the moment when Kennedy finally ensures that Spencer's plan is fulfilled. Susan attempts to telephone the prison governor with the news that Garrett is guilty, but, overcome by emotion, is unable to do so. Kennedy places the phone back on the hook, and there is a cut back to the governor's office, where Garrett is being pardoned. The phone rings, the governor answers, the pardon is cancelled. Presumably Kennedy has persuaded Susan to try again. This second phone call from which the sight of the caller is repressed inevitably recalls the first (Patti Grey's to Garrett), and marks the shift from disequilibrium to equilibrium, the narrative's *raison d'être.*

Spencer and Garrett's plan, the body of the narrative, ostensibly opposes fact to fiction, attempts to reverse the meaning of appearances, to prove definitively that appearances do not equal truth. But the enterprise is based on the essential paradox that they can only do this by offering as truth an alternative set of appearances/representations, in the form of the photographs which are Spencer's record of their evidence-planting activities. The revelation of Garrett's guilt means that the 'truth', the meaning, of the photographs is reversed. What has been depicted within the text is the representation of that guilt. Importantly, the denial of any psychological dimension in terms of character means that the film is concerned obsessively with the ambiguous status of its own images, into which are constantly introduced heavily marked instances of specularity and representation. The way in which the meta-discourse of the film text is intertwined with, but separate from, the method of the plan is made clear when Garrett and Spencer first visit the Club Zombie, Patti Grey's workplace. The scene opens with a shot of a sign bearing the club's name, flanked by two wooden cut-out female figures. The camera tracks towards the 'Burlesque' sign, and then up to the pictures advertising the dancing girls inside. The movement and object of the shot is then balanced by, and opposed to, the actions of the depicted characters. As the camera is tracking in from the left, Garrett and Spencer walk into frame from the right, and the camera's gaze at the photographs is doubled by Spencer pointing to the images of the girls who shared Patti Grey's dressing room.

From this point on it is a case of image within image within image . . . One of the dancers describes Garrett as a 'doll', which is followed by a dissolve to an outfitter's shop where he, dressed in a coat similar to that worn by the murderer, is gazing at his own image, reflected in a mirror.

Beyond a Reasonable Doubt: image (making) within . . .

. . . image

Garrett is then photographed by Spencer, with the latter also reflected in the mirror, and his image included in the photograph he is taking. Dolly Moore is shown making herself up in front of a mirror, in which she and Garrett are reflected as they arrange their date. A shot of Dolly and Garrett embracing dissolves into a close-up of a newspaper photograph showing the two of them 'dining out'. Spencer photographs Garrett at the scene of the murder, holding a newspaper. He moves closer to Garrett in order to include the date on the newspaper, a movement opposed to the sudden cut to a high-angle shot of the two of them, at the moment when the picture is taken. A close-up, from Spencer's point of view, then shows the Polaroid camera being opened up, and Garrett's image being removed. Similarly Spencer is shown photographing Garrett at the wheel of his car, followed by a close-up, this time from Garrett's point of view, of the resulting image. When Garrett takes Dolly back to the club he deliberately sets himself up as the object of the girl Terri's look, hoping that she will recognise the hat and coat he is wearing. On two occasions Garrett refers to images from outside the space of the film-text in order to explain his knowledge of certain facts. He claims to know the colour of Patti Grey's hair, because 'her picture was all over the newspapers', and later tells Spencer that he recognises the murder spot because he has seen newspaper photographs of it.

Garrett's arrest is conceived in terms of a switch. Having been the object of the gaze of the Law (PS represented by Spencer), he is now

Tom Garrett on trial: 'framed' (*Beyond a Reasonable Doubt*)

The look . . .

watched by Kennedy (representative of ʟs). As Kennedy tells Dolly:
'We'll be watching you every minute.' As the murder is about to be
re-enacted, re-presented, the image becomes multi-framed. A shot, from
Garrett's point of view, shows the police car which is following them,
framed in the rearview mirror. The mirror itself is framed within the car
windshield, which is in turn framed within the film frame itself. All in all
a fitting climax to Spencer's attempt to 'frame' Garrett for the Patti Grey
killing.

   Garrett's trial is depicted as an extension of their plan — the images
representing the events themselves contain the depiction of a process of
representation. Cameras are shown filming within the courtroom. When
Dolly Moore is called to the stand the tracking movement of a camera is
shown, presumably following her movement, but she herself is not seen.
Parts of the trial are shown in the form of television broadcasts, with the
television image framed within the film image. The language of the trial,
the notion of an 'exhibit', becomes an ironic reflection of the inability of
film ('language') to show 'truth'. The more that objects such as the
cigarette lighter and match-book are displayed in close-up as 'evidence',
the more their 'meaning', what they prove, becomes arbitrary. The
equivalence of the two representations/constructions of Garrett's guilt,
the framing and the trial, is stressed when Spencer is killed. What his
death signifies is the loss of the images proving Garrett's innocence (the
photographs are burnt in his car), and as he leaves in his car before the

120

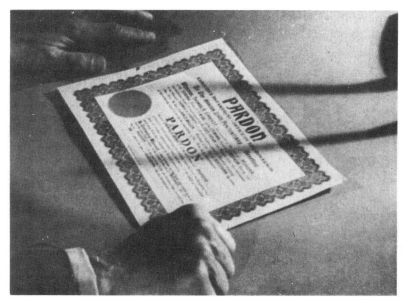

. . . and the object it is denied (*Beyond a Reasonable Doubt*)

The law claims its victim (*Beyond a Reasonable Doubt*)

fatal collision the trial is presented at that moment in terms of loss of image. It is present only on the soundtrack in the form of a report on the car radio.

Subsequent events duplicate, mirror and sometimes reverse the body of the narrative, in a condensed form. The plan to prove Garrett's innocence is mirrored by the efforts of Susan, literally 'taking the place of' Spencer, to save him through the investigations carried out by the newspapermen. The accumulated evidence collected by Spencer, and destroyed with him, is doubled by the contents of the envelope left for the District Attorney. The 'guilty' verdict pronounced by the court is replaced by the shot of the newspaper headline 'Garrett is Innocent'. The denial of Garrett's claims about the pictures ('They're just remnants of photographs. They could be pictures of anything') is replaced by acceptance ('Garrett has been telling the truth').

But as the text has constantly denied its own ability to represent 'truth' as opposed to 'appearance', it is inevitable that it should not resolve itself by such a neat assertion of 'truth' over 'falsehood'. What destroys Garrett is an assertion of himself as subject, a reference to his past life, a time outside the present of the text within which he has been the stressed *object* of a variety of discourses. When he speaks the name Emma, he refers to a state of subjectivity where the subject/object split, with regard to himself and Emma, was taken to its logical (Langian) conclusion: he killed her. But this past must be repressed from the narrative in order that a mystery, a question, a gap to be filled, may be posited. Garrett's execution (like the murder of Emma, outside the space of the text) is the simple, logical, inevitable conclusion of the subject/object split acted out across the textual representation — that between the Law (LS/PS) and Garrett. The 'twists' (innocent then guilty then innocent then guilty) make the status of what is represented ambiguous, but only in terms of a 'truth' which lies outside, is repressed from, what is shown. It is no accident that Garrett betrays himself by a slip of the tongue, a spoken word which refers back to this 'truth', rather than visually.

In fact, at the end of the film Garrett attempts, unsuccessfully, to assert his subjectivity in terms of the look finding its object. The prison governor's instruction to 'Take Garrett back to his cell' is followed by a shot of Garrett looking down at the pardon he has now been denied. There is then a cut to a close-up of the pardon lying on the desk between the governor's hands, followed in turn by a cut back to Garrett looking, i.e. the 'classic' construction of a point of view shot. But not only is Garrett denied the pardon (what the sequence of shots signifies), he is also denied the subjectivity (point of view) for which he strives — he is looking out of frame to the right, but the pardon itself is seen in close-up from the left of the frame. In other words the editing construction hints at a subjectivity that is actually not realised.

This moment from *Beyond a Reasonable Doubt* is a perfect example of Raymond Bellour's 'distance between desire and its object', where desire is synonymous with the gaze. But the object of desire is here a document, rather than the human form, a clear and simple pointer to the fact that *Beyond a Reasonable Doubt*, together with *Testament of Dr Mabuse*, is Lang's most 'abstract' film, with a heavy emphasis on, and investigation of, the problem of the status of 'what meets the eye'. It must be emphasised that the cost of this abstraction is the repression of the significant female presence — the unproblematic Lilli in the earlier film, here the dead Patti Grey, doubled by Dolly, and the rejected Susan Spencer.

And this in turn makes all the more apparent the extent to which the other narratives discussed here hinge on the dramatised investigation of the female, as well as the significance of the male/subject-female/object relation within the terms of a patriarchal order/equilibrium, which it is the aim of each narrative to attain. The often noted 'bleakness' of the endings of certain Lang movies (*You Only Live Once, Scarlet Street, Rancho Notorious, The Big Heat*), seen as working against a Hollywood grain, is the direct result of a failure to attain this specific equilibrium. The contradiction between the quotes from Andrew Sarris and Claire Johnston at the beginning of this essay is actually no contradiction at all, since both viewpoints depend on the female being associated with the embodiment of a value. This can be positive/loving (Jo in *You Only Live Once*) or negative/destructive (Kitty in *Scarlet Street*). But the common factor of femaleness (otherness) which leads to the object of desire/ investigation effectively cancels out the difference between them. The trigger for the various narratives is that all the women embody the same difference.

For any 'man-subject behind the camera' the steady gaze at the female figure effectively constitutes an absence of narrative. Ophuls' cinema, according to Paul Willemen, is the dramatisation of precisely such a desire to look. If one attempts to examine the marks of 'Lang' using the same terms, the text, and the individual narratives which comprise it, emerges placed firmly under the signs of repression. Philippe Demonsablon suggests an opposition between what drives Lang's narratives (for him, the will and the concept) and 'scenes of contemplation . . . usually favouring female characters'. The idea of repression, the difference in stylistic tendencies between Ophuls and Lang, is exactly the feeling of the gaze being 'turned towards some elsewhere', the possibility of a robot, a portrait, a brooch, etc.

The naturalisation of mainstream cinema's narrative discourse involves the naturalisation of a seamless system of looking, whereby the gaze of the spectator is smoothly relayed through the gazes of characters within the diegesis at other characters. The major importance of the Lang-text is that, as a whole, it represents a radical dramatisation of the processes of vision and discourse, and therefore works against this

123

naturalisation. This is the area approached by Bellour. But this dramatisation is only of interest when the individual narratives through which it occurs are considered in terms of the place and significance of women within those narratives. For only then do the terms desire, the gaze, style, narrative, etc., start to cohere around the name Lang, and the Lang-text become something other than a paranoid projection of a hopeless fatalism.

JEAN-LOUIS COMOLLI AND FRANÇOIS GÉRÉ

Two Fictions Concerning Hate

'*Do the great Hollywood films now address themselves to us only in the past tense, to those of us steeped in cinephilia? . . . Do they work as anything other than a collection of souvenirs, legends or fetishes? Or simply, do they still work for us, and on what basis could they function today in a manner that is not embalmed?*'

The questions asked at the beginning of the essay which follows, which appeared in Cahiers du Cinéma *no. 286, March 1978, can be read as addressed to* Cahiers' *own past, as exemplified by the Mourlet and Demonsablon essays reprinted in this volume. The essential shift marked by the questions is from a celebration/investigation of the subject, 'the legend' of Lang, to an investigation of the use value of the texts signed by him. In the preceding chapter an attempt was made to bring together the areas of the identifiable 'systems of vision' in the Lang text, and the question of the significance of women within the repeated Oedipal trajectories of various narratives within that text. Here the opposition is between the ostensible, seemingly obvious, ideological project of a Hollywood 'propagandist' fiction, and the peculiar inflection exercised upon and within that fiction by the marks of 'Lang', usefully summarised as 'making the spectator pay for his place'. This opposition makes possible a reading of the text against what appears to be its grain. The essay can therefore perhaps be most usefully seen as an attempt to reconstruct* Hangmen Also Die *as a 'category (e) film', according to the categories proposed by Comolli and Paul Narboni in their important article 'Cinema/Ideology/Criticism' (*Cahiers du Cinéma, *no. 216, October 1969, translated in* Screen, *Summer 1971). Films in category (e) are those 'which seem at first sight to belong firmly within the (dominant) ideology and to be completely under its sway, but which turn out to be so only in an ambiguous manner . . . there is a noticeable gap, a dislocation, between the starting point and the finished product . . . The films we are talking about throw up obstacles in the way of the ideology, causing it to swerve and get off course. The cinematic framework lets us see it, but also shows it up and denounces it . . . An internal criticism is taking place which cracks the film apart at the seams. If one reads the film obliquely, looking for symptoms; if one looks beyond its apparent formal coherence, one can see that it is riddled with cracks: it is splitting under an internal tension, which is simply not there in an ideologically innocuous film'.*

The fact that the above mentioned shift marks a certain displacement of 'Lang' is also of course indicated by this article's next point of reference, 'Lubitsch' . . .

The point of departure[1] was a number of questions. For instance: do the great Hollywood films now address themselves to us only in the past tense, to those of us steeped in cinephilia? Do they merely flaunt the golden age of a lost cinema, to the irritation of successors arriving too late? Do they work as anything other than a collection of souvenirs, legends or fetishes?[2] Or simply, do they still work for us, and on what basis could they function today in a manner that is not embalmed?

GERMANY BESIDE HERSELF

The point of departure was also two of these films, *Hangmen Also Die* and *To Be or Not to Be*, a curious yet logical association of two films long granted the status of masterpiece, viewed and viewed again, yet both rather lost from sight, neglected even for specialist revivals, or perhaps one should say passed over, the Lang because purists always saw it (wrongly) as tainted by a certain Brechtian *crudity*,[3] and the Lubitsch perhaps as being a little too malicious, a little too clever, a little too unscrupulous, a little too all of these things at once. One film is seen as a blemish on the (supposed) polish of Lang's filmography, and the other, in the airily massive and delicately brutal manner of so many Lubitsch films, as a blemish on the (supposedly) harmonious vista of 'Hollywood cinema', a brand label which has come in handy rather too often, in *Cahiers* as elsewhere, for stuffing widely divergent experiences and totally opposed methods into the same catch-all bag.

But it would be more to the point to talk of the impossible association of two fictions whose referents nevertheless converged. Referents? In

1. For a course organised [in December 1977] by the Centre Culturel at Valence and by Françoise Calvez, as part of a 'Cinema and History' programme which brought together representatives of some forty film societies belonging to the F.F.C.C., and during which we were able to view each of the two films twice in succession and then discuss them at length. The text which follows is a re-elaboration of these discussions: its origin and genesis are therefore collective. Furthermore, we (J.-L.C. and F.G.) have been working for some time on a book about Renoir's *La Marseillaise*, based on articles by J.-L.C. which have been or will be published in these pages, and on F.G.'s researches as a historian into the French Revolution as represented in films. The present text thus fits in to the overall context of a consideration of *historical fiction* (cf. *Cahiers* no. 278).

2. Or even: a collection of recipes. Except that it takes faith to make these recipes work, which means that they cannot simply be copied cynically (as is the case with today's young Hollywood lions), nor can they be imitated even though disparaged (as is the case with leftist fiction film-makers).

3. Brecht's violent and bitter notes in his 'Journal de Travail' (L'Arche) should be read in this connection. On Brecht's own admission, apart from the opening sequence (Heydrich's outburst against the sabotage in the Skoda factories), nothing of his 'collaboration' survives in the final script. The notes reveal the extent to which Lang wanted nothing to do with Brecht's ideas, and to which Brecht misunderstood Lang's work. We shall be quoting some of these notes.

126

that respect one could hardly imagine a greater proximity (don't proximity, overlapping, similarity, always exist only in the area of referents anyway?). In one case Czechoslovakia, in the other Poland. Not only two neighbouring countries in central Europe, but two countries which, viewed from Hollywood (or from Berlin), occupy the same situation as the small nation falling prey to a bigger one. Two democracies mopped up by the Nazi vacuum cleaner. Two countries with an ancient culture, two homes of *humanism*, afflicted by what Brecht insisted should not be called 'barbarism'. Another point in common: popular resistance against Nazi oppression. The war therefore, which in 1942 — the year when both films were started — the United States had just rather unwillingly entered.

For of course yet another referential reduplication places, at the intersection where the two fictions meet before diverging wildly, the common and dual adherence of both film-makers to the two rival nations (with all the ambiguous confederacy implied by rivalry). Germany as left by Lubitsch under the gravitational pull from Hollywood, as lost by Lang under the advance of Hitler; and America, attained by both and wishfully the victor. So this is not merely Germany seen from America as *different* from America (different from American *peace* and *democracy*), as for instance in Leo McCarey's *Once Upon a Honeymoon* (also 1942); it is Germany as referent, but this referent itself considered as already lost (the referent: what is lost en route). Both films are in effect about a Germany that is constantly *beside itself,* slipping out of its geographical limits and losing its moral temper: unbridled. And at the same time, what this evil Germany has overlaid and crushed is none other than that lost soul of old Europe, culture and feelings, art and the good life: it is in fact precisely what the *good* Germany could be. Through referential contamination, the spread of Nazi Germany through all of the old Europe produces the identification of Poland or Czechoslovakia with pre-Nazi Germany.

This referential identification operates all the more readily in that émigré European film-makers in Hollywood tended to refer American audiences (for whom these two films, like all others at the time, were primarily intended and virtually reserved)[4] back to the already classic and auto-referential image of the United States as a collection of fragments of old Europe. You are concerned, these two films seem to say to American audiences, because this fight is also about *you*, about the heredity that made you, about the referent for your values.

---

4. Closure of the European market to American films. The Nazi victories palpably weakened Hollywood.

These were militant days, and Hollywood was preoccupied with what one might call the open propaganda film, with propaganda both supercharging and explicitly defining its usual ideological programming: there had been *Man Hunt*, also directed by Lang, Hawks' *Sergeant York*, the *Why We Fight* series, etc. This mobilisation of Hollywood was of course an attempt to sway public opinion in favour of the just war, to counter pacifist and isolationist tendencies by reminding Americans that they had (among others) a European heritage, by providing the great seminal myths of their society with a genealogy.

Also well known is the way Americans wavered in the face of Nazism, with relatively powerful pro-Nazi currents circulating (and even creating serious difficulties for those, like Chaplin, who denounced them), with Hitler himself and the notion of his regime exercising a considerable attraction (an attraction admirably illustrated by McCarey's engaging Nazi Baron and Lubitsch's irresistible Professor). The problem was to reverse this climate mildly or actively favourable to the Nazi atrocities and to impose a different image of these from the one they had contrived to pass off as true. Since Nazism had taken particular care over moulding its own presentation, it had to be taken over and repostulated in a counter-presentation which would brand the Nazi *mise en scène* as just that, a *mise en scène*: manipulation of appearance, bogus show, machination.

The war, at first, was waged not only by the war machines, but by the image machines as well. One system of representation against another. One representation dismantling the other in order to denounce it as evil (deceitful, dictatorial, monstrous: bestiality plus mechanisation), while at the same time establishing itself on the right side and annexing to itself the right values (truth, liberty, generosity: humanity, always humanity). So both films have their representation of Nazism and, as a corollary, of what it is not, of what resists and combats Nazism.

Propaganda, in Hollywood as elsewhere and as always in those days, did not merely assume a hateful enemy (accordingly given all the coded signs of negativity, including physical and mental taints). It assumed him to be, even at the height of his triumphs, resistible and vincible. He must of course arouse fear, horror, disgust, but in the final analysis there must be a touch of paper about the tiger. He must be both inflated and deflated, blown up with hatred and the balloon burst. We are halfway between a dialectical exercise and a conjuring trick. You don't believe it? Well, we'll show you! You really are convinced? Frankly, you don't need to be. This apparently contradictory logic of the propagandist discourse, which establishes power only to turn it into weakness, which proclaims the reversibility of violence and which turns terror up full only to damp it down again, is not so very far removed from the elementary mechanisms

128

of dramatic fiction. In each case the representation produced functions as a system of invocation and as a cathartic outburst. And the fictional aspect hinges on the *stake* behind the propaganda: that there must be *a* spectator to win over.

BUT SUPPOSE THE FICTION BETRAYED THE PROPAGANDA?

So the Nazi shadow is spreading over Europe? Czechoslovakia and Poland are occupied and oppressed? A propaganda film based on a denunciation of these barbarous acts would be defeating its purpose if it did not dramatise and incorporate *into its fiction* resistance to such acts, and successful resistance at that! Fighting back is not only desirable, it is possible, it has *already begun*. The hatred is immediately on the offensive. As so often in Hollywood message films, basically the audience is won over not on negative grounds (denunciation, critical condemnation), but *positive*: these resistants fighting against Nazism are fighting *for* your values, they embody *your* ideals (dignity, liberty, democracy, etc.), they are, in a word, the sort of heroes you love. 'Positive heroes', of course, because many more of that breed are to be found in American than in Russian or Chinese films.

All this, of course, is in keeping with the propagandist scheme, the programme allotted to our two fictions by social necessity: we shall be examining in detail how the fictions coped. One effect of this programming, not the least disconcerting for us today, remains to be noted: these propaganda films intervene precipitately (which is logical and necessary for their purpose) at the shortest possible distance from the referential events. History here is actual, contemporary with the two fictions which deal with it. So the referent literally encroaches. And yet, each in its own way, the two fictional machines proceed to drain it of its substance, to detach and distance it; not, in other words, extracting any of the ready-made effects it offers: effects of reality, authenticity, verisimilitude, appearance, not even historical effects, nothing. But wasn't the point, after all, for them to put an end to it?

HANGMEN ALSO DIE or: The victims are much like the executioners

Machine against machine, we said. Here it is in fact a machination successfully directed against the Nazi machine. The latter secreting the former, which in turn throws it out of gear. It all begins *moderato,* just as the leading citizens of Prague are making obeisance and swearing allegiance to the gauleiter Heydrich, with the discovery that things are not going smoothly at the Skoda factories. Annexed to the service of the German war machines, the works are the object of organised sabotage. Heydrich denounces a conspiracy of darkness, a plot by unknown hands, a machination. The Czech workers are obstructing production. They are

129

circulating airy leaflets which show tortoises lounging around, urging idleness. Their resistance is through corrosion: the corrosions of humour and of adopting the line of least resistance. They do not take the situation seriously. A strong sense of discordance is aroused between, on the one hand, the grave funereal pomp of the Nazi ceremonial and the deliberate solemnity, the *tragic seriousness* with which Heydrich's authority is presented, and on the other these absurd, Disney-ish images of tortoises folding their arms, which nevertheless play the role of the grain of sand that gums up the works. It's intolerable, Heydrich roars, in substance saying that the machines must operate at full productivity or lives will answer for it, hostages will be taken, executions carried out.

THE LIE ACCELERATES

When we see Heydrich again he is dead, indeed embalmed. But his first and only appearance weighs heavily. The character is designed by the fiction to contrive within a single scene, to convene and concentrate in his person, through his body, his face, his attitude, the signs of a radical negativity, everything necessary to make him instantly and eternally hateful to the spectator. This body, this voice, these eyes bear death, castration, abnormality, sexual ambiguity. No hint of amiability; quite the contrary, in fact, something equivocal, venomous, petty even in his extremes of cruelty. Heydrich is conceived as a repellent Master, driven by domination-repulsion in tandem. And yet . . . he, and he alone, is given body in this scene. A body that is sexless and ageless, man-woman-child; but for that reason, in addition to the fact of his authority, an erotic body. This is a privilege granted to none of the other people present in the scene, puppets in frock coats or uniforms, bodies purely as a matter of form. But what does this lead to? What is the effect of this erotic identification of the Nazi figure?[5] The answer is revealed by the impossible face to face confrontation between the incarnation of the new masters and the representative of the old. Under the very nose of a *one-eyed* Czech general, Heydrich drops his cane, stares fixedly, and waits. Perturbation in the general, who is literally not equipped to meet this stare, a cripple forced to publicly acknowledge and witness a repeat performance of his emasculation. He submits, bends down, picks up the cane, and hands it to *his* master, who is gratified. If this confirms that bodies and sensual gratification, whether or not they can be commanded, is what it is all about, it also tells us those who are on the side of death, and that 'one cannot look death in the face'. What this establishes therefore, as the film's programme, is the great Langian symbolic system which equates the look with death, the wish with failure, gratification

5. Here we have one of the earliest examples, if not the prototype, of the eroticisation of the Nazi figure which was to be widely exploited by the European (and especially Italian) cinema in the 1970s.

with castration, which echoes a metaphysic of fall and punishment, but also, more particularly, launches an economy of loss, a mechanism of negation, a circulation of flight and pursuit enabling the fiction to progress.

Even before we learn that Heydrich has been killed (although we really hardly need to be told of the assassination, so aware have we been made of his link with death), the characters are introduced to us as already caught up in the logic of deceit, already *at fault*. We see someone hiding, running away, exchanging his workman's cap for a bourgeois felt hat,[6] someone who has something (himself) to hide: this is Dr Svoboda, Heydrich's assassin. And we see someone who sees him running away (Mascha Novotny), a chance witness (nothing is chance in Lang's films) and a reluctant one (but it is she who looks, so . . .) of a sin (original) which she knows nothing of. It is enough that she saw and that we saw her see: admirable and terrifying logic of the Langian *découpage*, which sutures the character's viewpoint to that of the spectator and makes us recipients of the trap to which they are predestined by the fiction. For the fiction here starts and functions as a trap, and it is they, the resistants and their accomplices, who are caught in it at the beginning, while we spectators — as we shall see — end as its victims. So Mascha Novotny, who has seen what she was (not) meant to see, succumbs to the principle of deceit, being in possession of a truth which she begins by hiding (sending the soldiers who are after Svoboda off in the wrong direction, on a false *trail*), although she can only conjecture this truth since she knows nothing as yet of the assassination. A truth which subsequently, even when she wants to, she can no longer admit. Always the lie accelerates, remains stronger than the (guilty) conscience. As for this first lie, apparently anodyne, innocent (but the only innocents in this film are those who foreclose on truth) and in a sense 'positive', an act of ordinary, everyday resistance and of an instinctive modicum of sympathy for the

---

6. A metaphorical figuration of the shift within the fiction from popular resistance (the Skoda workers) to a resistance by the elite: Dr Svoboda, Professor Novotny, etc. Similarly, when the Nazis call the roll of the hostages they have taken, there is only one worker among a list of teachers, lawyers, doctors, etc. This was obviously not intended by Brecht, who wanted to call the film *Trust the People*, and who wrote: 'Who can tell the infinite dreariness of this sort of trash, the film about hostages I have to work on now? All this murk and imbroglio and phoniness! What little decency there is peters out because I am strictly limited to the framework of a national-bourgeois uprising' (p. 309). And a little further on (14/9/42), when he decides to write an 'ideal script' to submit to Lang, he notes: 'Naturally I chiefly emphasise the scenes with the people' (p. 319).

Reality, however — although of course Brecht and Lang did not know this — had given its ironical casting vote between their points of view. It was learned later that the assassination of Heydrich had been carefully planned outside Czechoslovakia (in Britain) by a military commando whose members, while in action in Prague, were *disguised as workmen*. The Czech resistance was not too pleased about this commando operation from outside whose consequences they had to suffer on their own.

weak against the strong, this justifiable initial lie solicits both our sympathy and our complicity (we are already unable to like the Nazis any more and ready to love the resistants). And at the same time it sets in motion the whole mechanism of successive lies which become increasingly oppressive and ensnaring.

BEYOND A REASONABLE DOUBT

This is so because a lie here, whatever the (valid) reasons for it, is the negative token of the truth, its mark if not its letter. Moreover, the more 'valid' these reasons may seem (positive aspirations, decent or noble sentiments, emotional impulses), the more ineluctably they lead the people who subscribe to them to suffer the negative effects of their relationship to the truth as the thing that is causing their punishment and undoing. In the Langian system, the truth is what kills, what condemns to death[7] — if only that symbolic death with which the tacked-on happy endings have to content themselves. Whether they speak out or keep quiet, the characters in the fiction who know the truth (a secret they always share with the spectator, who is the first to know) fall helplessly into the trap of an impossible choice between two versions of death.

To reveal this truth is to reveal it to the Germans, and thus not only send Heydrich's assassin to his death but nip the entire popular resistance in the bud in so far as it has just acceded to symbolic power by inflicting this death on the Nazi machine. Silence must therefore be maintained, the name of the assassin concealed, and the ranks of the resistance rallied round him. But to maintain silence also means sending hundreds of hostages to their deaths: well aware of the symbolic implications of this assassination of their leader, the Germans interpret it correctly as a challenge hurled against them by an entire populace. So they round on the people and return the challenge: accept or die. An impossible choice: either the life of one man as against the lives of many, or else the lives of many as against the death of a symbol.

Lang's malevolence is to record this old debate about the relative importance of lives and ideas, about individual sacrifice and collective responsibility, precisely from the one viewpoint which precludes any solution: that of the American spectator to be won over to the cause of the anti-Nazi struggle (the point of the exercise), a spectator assumed to be humanist, democratic and liberal, and *necessarily* assumed to be so since it is on the basis of these ideological qualities that he is to be mobilised against Nazi barbarism and inhumanity. This point of view is moreover

---

7. Think of the irresistible mechanisms of, for instance, *Fury, You Only Live Once* or *Beyond a Reasonable Doubt*: evidence always insufficient, impossible to produce, or worse, reversible; innocence such that it tumbles into culpability; the truth elusive except through death.

represented by the fiction in the arguments it initiates both in the Novotny family circle and among the people of Prague. The purpose throughout is to allow identification with the oppressed Czechs.[8]

If the resistance yields to this humanist pressure which is exercised both within the fiction and in the auditorium, if it hands over Svoboda or allows him to surrender himself to the Germans as he nobly proposes (the positive hero must still be maintained), it renounces itself as a force, undermines itself as a machine, loses its credibility while stressing the Nazi supremacy. A suicidal solution. But not to hand over Svoboda means condemning the hostages, and by so doing becoming an accessory to the Nazi death-machine. It also means coming to resemble it, adopting its totalitarian logic which favours the social machine over men's lives. This is to bring discredit on the cause they represent. An impossible solution. Either lose the advantage of a good public image. Or adopt a bad one. A fictional stratagem, a trick, will be needed to get out of the trap. As we shall see.

None of the people who know this secret, which is becoming an increasingly heavy burden to carry, will therefore ever be in a position to reveal it, even if tempted. The resistance leaders, for the reason just given: to preserve the symbol (though to preserve it means turning it upside-down). Dr Svoboda, because the logical mechanism that has been established forbids it: he *is* the symbol, so his life no longer belongs to him, and neither does the option of death. A runaway, an exile from his element, an embarrassing presence, a focus for drama and suspense, this is all Svoboda is. Professor Novotny, because he stands for the Code, for the Principle, for transcendental Values. He knows, before his daughter tries to tell him; he even forbids her to do so: the secret is both something that is shared by all and something that cannot be shared. The Principle, therefore.[9] And since his daughter insists, since the secret

8. This identification — purely ideological — is possible only if the Czech community is represented as split by the question of the hostages in a supposed reflection of American public opinion: it is the identity of the split which supports the homology between the group represented and the spectator group. However, this mass debate on the question of the hostages, which *must* necessarily be represented to induce identification, is also what threatens the resistance with disintegration in the fiction, breaching its ideological unity. After having been dangled, it must therefore vanish from the scene. The function of the stratagem whereby *the wrong man* is handed over to the Nazis is to suppress this awkward debate, to show a people and a resistance united above and beyond, and in spite of, the split.

9. Just as the Nazis arrive to take him hostage, Professor Novotny is concluding a lecture on the American Declaration of Independence to some of his students! Thus, through him, the Nazis are attacking the great American values. Crude; yet it was through the use of such artless enormities that American propagandist fictions could play the innocent, the positive hero, without the subtle precautions and ingenuities imposed by bad conscience, without heed to referential truth. Their strength derives from the fact that they annex what would constitute their adversaries' best argument without the slightest hesitation: they cannot be reproached for what they openly assume and display with a sort of tranquil immodesty: yes, the model for all democracy is American, yes, the Czech heroes are inspired by the Declaration of Independence . . .

133

is an intolerable burden and she must speak of it (and who better to entrust it to, entailing fewer risks, than her father?), he tells her again: No one must know. He opens a dictionary (the Book, the Bible, the Code) and makes her read the definition: 'No one, no person, nobody.' Not even himself, who already knows in the knowledge that this truth is fatal.

And finally Mascha Novotny, a figure of irresolution, representing the average conscience which seeks and doubts, the very image of the Langian heroine, appointed prey to a malign destiny which makes her pay dearly for believing she still has desires in a world of obligations. More than any of the others she is pulled and tossed about, simultaneously trapped by the necessity and the impossibility of choice (between falsehood and truth, good cause and clear conscience, as well as between her fiancé and the inescapable Svoboda, whose lover she must pretend to be). The first time she tries to unburden herself of the secret to her father. The second, she gets as far as the Gestapo HQ and stops there, for no other reason than the Langian logic which insists that one does not betray when one wants to, one betrays when one does not want to (as indeed is what happens). The third time, on the point of confessing to her fiancé the deceit she has been forced to carry out — by which he too has been taken in — she is again prevented from doing so by the presence behind the door of Gruber of the secret police, the man who *wants* that truth. She is therefore obliged to add instead to the falsehood, giving it a new lustre, a renewed strength. And loses the fiancé.

On the other hand are those who know nothing, and in order to find out, indulge in a frenzy of investigations, interrogations, snares, threats, blackmail by hostage, and finally executions. Lang does not lump all the members of the Gestapo together in the same bag. Nearly all of them are to one side, only one on the other. Nearly all of them are cogs in the death machine, supercharged with Nazi negativity, uniforms, arrogance, brutality, stupidity. These are never to know who killed Heydrich. They batter against a wall of silence. They fall into every pitfall. They are fooled and flouted by the great machination of the resistance. Blind from beginning to end, especially when they think they see, mired in total misunderstanding and ultimately impotent, they are very evidently the predestinate losers in this prearranged game. Truth escapes them as a matter of principle. Access to it is denied them not so much because they are so obviously on the wrong side (as we shall see, there is no *right* side in the film's scheme) as because they are represented as *inhuman. As mechanisms which do not think, simply as props for hatred.*

A NAZI READER OF FICTION

And then there is Gruber of the secret police, he too a member of the Gestapo but devoid of uniform or ritual. He does not give the automatic 'Heil Hitler' salute. He makes no profession of Nazism. With his bowler hat and shabby suit, he is the classic detective straight out of *Mabuse*. If he is so concerned with the truth, it is for its own sake, and not for any political reason or from practical necessity. He considers the secret as a *challenge* which must be fully accepted. His concern is with the external signs of reality. What resists him is also what stimulates him and urges him on. Unlike the other characters as a whole, Nazis and resistants alike, who are carried along by a logic stronger than they are which goes beyond them, cuts through them, manipulating them and fitting them to its purpose, Inspector Gruber fights back, attempting to swim against the current of appearances, lies, concocted solutions. He is, one might say, one of the few who effectively *resist*, one of the few that the film shows actually doing so — along with a few populist figures like the woman street vendor — and certainly more actively than the resistance workers who occupy the limelight but who are not seen actually resisting at all (one does not see, remember, Svoboda's assassination of Heydrich). Of course this is a play on words: what sort of *resistance* are we talking about? Some resist the Nazis by elaborating lies, by laying false trails. Gruber works for the Nazis and only resists false trails. Gruber, secret policeman and member of the Gestapo, is naturally on the wrong side, the resistants on the right side. Or so, at least, the conventional starting-point of the film confidently assumes; the work of the fiction, on the other hand . . .

More than any of the other characters, the fiction makes us accompany Gruber in his patient, tortuous quest for truth. But since we know this truth from the beginning, we spectators have a considerable start over him. And we watch him close this gap with both anxiety and some satisfaction. Anxiety in so far as Gruber's progress introduces the suspense of a chase: will he unmask the culprit, tear aside the veil of lies, destroy the heroes? But also a muted satisfaction, a sense of relief: at last in this fiction, among all these machines, an intelligence is at work, another mode of functioning has burst in, a character has broken free. His investigation tells us nothing we do not already know. But by accompanying him, by following this sort of initiatory journey in his wake, we learn, as he does, the meaning of this truth that is finally unveiled and the price that is to be paid for it: death, *his* death. And our death a little bit, too, since Gruber has for a time been our most direct representative in the fiction. Like us, Gruber is a reader of fiction.

In the first place, Gruber is endowed with a *body*: which distinguishes him sharply from the Nazis, as machines, but also from the resistants as phantoms, zombies. There are few physical effects in the film (or in Lang's work in general); the fiction produces none, and does not need to, quite the contrary. Its chief concern is that its most 'positive' heroes, those who represent the great values (justice, innocence, liberty, etc.), and who for that reason are plunged into an infernal cycle of events, should have as few physical traits as possible: should ultimately be no more than simulacra of bodies moved by a force, an energy, a logic which they do not understand and against which they are helpless. For their supreme determination and manipulation, they are better disincarnate. This is undoubtedly the case with the Novotnys. The father: pious image, symbol of an Idea. The daughter: abstract magnetic force, furrowed and gnawed by the secret working within her, dedicated to simulacra, image of censorship, of the suppression of instincts and desires. Her fiancé: now-always castrated, extinct body, force nil. As for Dr Svoboda, his body may be described as phantasmal; first because the logic of deceit in which he is trapped forces him to hide this body all the time, to attempt its dissimulation, or purely and simply its annulment: from the very first moment he *must not have been seen*, his visibility is even denied, he has become a negative presence. But phantasmal also because he has, quite literally, a *double*.[10] Retrospectively, a split presence runs through the fiction. Here again: simulacrum and snare. Snares of the body for all these purveyors of snares. Shadows which the fiction throws out, shadows in the true sense made by extraordinarily skilful lighting, pockets of darkness, light, matter and energy inverted.

Physical impressions are concentrated on a few 'secondary' characters[11] who are also, with the exception of the woman street vendor, representing the tortured body of the people, 'negative'. The polymorphous body of Heydrich, very soon embalmed. The imposing then shrivelled, insolent then cowed body of the brewer Czaka. And the body of Gruber. As we have noted, Gruber's position in the system precludes any identification with him: it is forbidden to identify with a Gestapo agent. However, as we have seen, his character-function as reader or decoder of fictional signifiers has a contrary tendency to identify his course with our own, to have him mirror us. The reversal of perspective (exclusion/inclusion) is accomplished largely under the impact of physical effects which the character piles up in a sort of frenzy of vitality, of instinctual energy which distinguishes him from everyone else (he hustles, eats, drinks, smokes, screws, sleeps, is constantly dressing and undressing, makes a spectacle of himself in his rage, explodes), as if he were attracting to himself all the matter wanting in the other characters. And this is in effect what happens at each confrontation between this excessively physical presence, this ball of matter and energy, and either the Nazi uniform-machines or the zombie-resistants. The mere physical presence of Gruber face to face with members of either group in a shot produces an effect of such violent contrast that his corporal reality, and their unreality, is stressed and accentuated: his

10. Dr Svoboda has indeed a *double*, fictionalised and represented as such: same appearance, same clothes, same profession. And who in fact stands in for him at the hospital while he is killing Heydrich.

11. One might advance the hypothesis that ultimately there are no secondary characters in the Langian fiction, or that all of them are secondary inasmuch as they only intervene to take part when the fiction requires them as pawns in its manoeuvrings.

power, their impotence. This aggressive body denotes as such these simulacra surrounding it. There is in Gruber a healthy vampire-growth which leaves the others anaemic.

A KISS CAN HIDE ANOTHER

All this comes over clearly and unmistakably in the celebrated scene where Gruber, on the track of the wounded resistance leader, arrives to search Mascha Novotny's room. Of course he is met by a *mise en scène* (still the same one): scantily dressed (though this still does not emphasise their bodies), Dr Svoboda and Mascha Novotny are staging a love scene. Gruber, of course, is the only member of the Gestapo never to have believed in their liaison: how could he (or we) believe that desire has been communicated between one absence of body and another? And our disbelief is even greater than his since we witnessed the disposition of the simulacrum.[12] He does not believe despite the pains taken by the simulators, who are forced by the logic of deceit to pile up *evidence*, verbal (a fake declaration of love for the benefit of the Gestapo microphone), visual (tender looks and poses), and even material. There, for instance, on Dr Svoboda's cheek, is the imprint of Mascha Novotny's lips. Damning evidence.

Taking in at a glance the implications of this pretty tableau, Gruber nevertheless remains reticent; he is not entirely convinced. And we spectators, who have witnessed both the genesis of the *mise en scène* and the inadequacy of its effects, can only agree with him: he is right to be sceptical. The Gruber-spectator identification takes shape following these impressions of bodies present or absent, whole or lacking. Here Gruber's body carries *our* conviction that the other bodies are missing from their element. And the anxiety caused by the situation owes less to suspense, to the imminent danger that the truth may be discovered (literally: with the curtain being lifted) along with the hidden body, and the heroes (who are less and less *ours*) betrayed; no, it springs rather from the unease shared by Gruber and ourselves when faced with this laborious *mise en scène* of inadequate bodies. These bodies feigning love are icy. They are at once cold, clean, glazed. There is death between them as there is in the scene, in the secret the scene holds, behind the curtain. Death which freezes the two simulacra-bodies, death which kills behind the curtain; death represented on stage by the simulacra, death personified in the wings by the body of the resistance leader whose blood is draining from him.

Gruber lifts his hat and scratches his head: the tableau that meets his

12. Several earlier scenes made us witnesses and accessories to this disposition of the simulacrum, notably the one in which Dr Svoboda and Mascha Novotny realise that they are being eavesdropped by Gestapo microphones and begin *acting*: roles which they are then unable to abandon, a union in deceit that is more binding than any other.

eyes is entirely consistent. Nothing is missing: the state of undress, the couch, the tender gestures, the kiss, even the embarrassment of the actors. He has surprised an amorous couple. And yet something in Gruber resists all this evidence. As happens each time he comes up against simulacra, Gruber takes a detour through materiality. Dr Svoboda, still on edge, busily pours out a couple of glasses of wine. In passing, Gruber remarks on — stresses for our benefit — something in the nature of a marked class distinction: it is the bourgeoisie, the refined in taste, who drink wine; he, Gruber, cruder and more plebeian, prefers the poor man's drink, beer. But this wine, a pointer to class, is about to find a use. We, like Dr Svoboda, see that blood (the blood of the resistance) is trickling drop by drop from the dying man in his hiding-place. Suddenly, under Gruber's very eyes, a signifier (or even a symbol) too many, heterogeneous to the simulacrum and threatening to destroy it, is defacing the tableau: matter and life have entered a *mise en scène* that cannot tolerate them. They must be wiped out, they too must be hidden (like the truth, like the hidden body). Dr Svoboda immediately improvises another stratagem, restoring the consistency of the simulacrum by obscuring the involuntary signifiers: he spills wine over the blood. A pool of wine on the pool of blood: perfect camouflage. That is the advantage of being bourgeois when one is a resistant: working-class beer would not have hidden the blood.[13]

The trick is successful: Gruber leaves. But before leaving, staging a scene in his turn, he sends for someone with the aid of whom he hopes to test the authenticity of the love scene, the truth of the performance he has witnessed: Mascha Novotny's fiancé. A typical police manoeuvre, this confrontation fails: yes, Mascha Novotny repudiates her fiancé, and yes, the simulacrum wins out over reality, deceit over truth. Unless it succeeds in another sense: which is to prove to us, as to Gruber, that there is certainly nothing going on between these bodies, that Mascha Novotny's supposed love for her fiancé was probably no different in kind from the love she simulates with Dr Svoboda, that nothing is broken up in the violence of this performance because there *is* nothing. Reversibility of these representations, which expose themselves even as they make their exposition.

Gruber's resistance to snares is linked both to the physical consistency of his body and to his openness (consumption — gratification — decipherment) to the persistence of the signifier. As a good policeman he is an adept at significant materiality, a reader of the polysemy of signs. His role in the fiction identifies the spectator's in this sense too, redistributing and formalising it; for if the spectator always has a start on Gruber, is in the know before him, he does not necessarily know

13. Cf. note 6. The resistance (in the film) became almost entirely a matter for the elite. There is some irony in having a Gestapo agent remark on the fact.

everything about the systems of signs which exhibit this knowledge and cause it to circulate. The knowledge we already possess by virtue of the position of (relative) mastery in which we are placed by the fiction, information given us *gratis* by the fiction and for which we do not have to work, on which we expend no energy, all this Gruber teaches us to view actively, to reacquire it, this time paying the price, measuring the resistances that set in and the effort required to overcome them, visualising for ourselves the work we did not have to do. He gives us a lesson in reading which contrasts an acquired, problematic mastery with the comfortable, institutional one.

Leaving with Mascha Novotny's former fiancé after the fiasco of the confrontation, Gruber perseveres but in vain. Nothing satisfies him, but nothing affords him a purchase either. In yet another detour through materiality (and probably a subtle policeman's ploy as well), he encourages the stricken fiancé to forget his troubles and proposes an orgy. The two men embark on a night of beer and prostitutes. Meanwhile the resistants' machination is closing in on its prey, the brewer Czaka, who is both guilty and a scapegoat; a collaborator with the Germans, offering them assistance and handing over resistants, he is denounced in a conspiracy by the entire town as being Heydrich's assassin. One by one his alibis have fallen apart, his witnesses have dissociated themselves, or worse, inculpated him further. Only Gruber could still clear him. But Gruber has disappeared. Not at Gestapo HQ, missing from his room, he is not to be found in any of the expected places. And in the morning, as the prostitutes leave — not without revealing in passing the obvious impotence of the fiancé, who, gloomier than ever, is brooding over his castration — Gruber rouses himself from his sleep and almost immediately finds the missing clue to the truth. The night is not without its hand in this, nor is the body, materiality, and probably sleep; something in the order of the unconscious is revealed by their alliance. We are also alerted to this by Gruber's physicality; the resistance it offers to the traps set by visible evidence tells us that this policeman does not function only through intellect, rational logic and deduction, and that he is not driven like the other characters by a principle which programmes him from head to foot while robbing him of his own substance: in other words, that there is a subjective element to the character.[14] And Gruber thereby acquires a further power of attraction which would make us identify with him were this not totally prohibited by referential pressure and by the barrier of a politico-moral super-ego. There is no question but

14. Another thing that distinguishes Gruber from all the other characters is that he asks himself questions and persists in trying to find answers. Of course this persistence, in obedience to the harsh Langian law, leads him to disaster, but it is also what shows us that there is something *unprogrammed* in him, something which in fact upsets and dismantles programming. That this sort of *creative* effervescence should be attributed to an agent working for the Nazis . . . heavens!

that Gruber belongs to the side that we are supposed to hate, and is even their ugliest customer. Yet the fictional artifice also makes him serve as our substitute, our image of physicality adheres to the image of his body, and we are sutured by the progressive organisation of his scrutiny.

THE LOOK RENDERED VISIBLE

The *découpage*, the perceptible process whereby the clue is discovered, discloses to us, the spectators, the mechanism of our implication. As so often in the great 'classic' fictions, a scene, a filmic moment, takes charge of the formal, almost didactic, *exposition* of the device which structures the fiction as a whole. For the spectator's benefit, the representation takes pains to present itself. The trap reveals how it works. Where the *découpage* kept our scrutiny ahead of Gruber's in the phony love scene by letting us see a pool of blood that remained invisible to him, here in this scene of waking after the night out a fusion between the two scrutinies takes place. The fiancé is sitting with his head in his hands, played out, brooding over his misfortunes. Gruber, slow and sluggish after his night out, is standing before a mirror. The fiancé sees traces of lipstick from one of the prostitutes on Gruber's cheek. He realises, even before we have had time to, that this is the mark of a *real* kiss, and that the one he saw the previous evening, planted by Mascha Novotny's lips on Dr Svoboda's cheek, was merely a skilful impression, a simulacrum. Suddenly his body, hitherto slumped, repudiated, swells expansively ; the blood of life flows back into him;[15] what he sees becomes visible. And this is in fact what Gruber sees in the mirror: the *intent* look of someone who has seen the truth, a physical impression which no longer fits the previous picture, a metamorphosis which remains inexplicable unless it is in himself, in Gruber as viewed by the other, that something essential has become visible. And that it is he, Gruber, who is carrying on himself what he has been looking for elsewhere. At the very second he sees the reflection of the fiancé's transformed body in the mirror, Gruber also sees reflected — and we see with him — the genuine imprint left by a mouth, by a real body: the form and outline of the lips are blurred, the effect is of a hurried, smeared trace, contrasting with the other sharp, clearly outlined impression. Matter wins out over line. The familiar and meaningless token from a body devoid of love wins out over the token feigned by a love devoid of a body. The fiancé can take heart: yes, he has been the victim of a snare; no, there never was any desire and the cherished body of his fiancée has never ceased to be asexual — just the opposite of the prostitute's crude, vulgar, sexualised body. This too is what Gruber immediately understands: where there is no body, there is a

15. It is difficult to avoid phallic metaphors precisely because this type of fiction, one of the countless variations of the Oedipal cultural archetype, evolves on the basis of a phallic axis..

snare; his own body is a refutation of the simulacrum; make-up does not mark all bodies in the same way because all bodies are not real, and so they are therefore not equivalent in their images, in their representation either; the images are deceitful, the representations alluring, they must be associated, compared, contrasted, in short they must be *read* in order to decide between them.

All this is conveyed to us by the duplication of the fiancé's body and his scrutiny, and of Gruber's body and his scrutiny, by the mirror. Direct and indirect representation combine together, redouble themselves, designate each other through an internal effect similar to the heraldic 'placing in the abyss' which also functions as a sign of the film's reflection on itself. Simultaneously we see:

— Gruber's body and marked face: which confronts us directly with the non-analogy (an image contains only false analogy, non-equivalence and non-identity, pseudo-resemblance: in other words, between an image and the thing, as between one image and another, there is a difference) between the two lipstick marks, the real one blurred and the remembered one distinct.

— The reflection of this body and face in the mirror (effect of inversion: here again reproduction means difference, the sameness is an impression), with in addition the reflection of Gruber's look at his own cheek, and therefore the course, perceptible to us, represented, taken by this look, by what brings eye, body and lipstick mark into association. Both the visible body and the look become visible. The passage through the mirror, through reflection, usually intensifying the impression of mirrored semblance, here functions as a reversal of appearances: one has to reach the real by way of the image; the denaturalisation of the visible, its designation as such, its self-representation and its reflex conceptualisation, means that the snares can be avoided, the simulacra rejected. (Another example in passing of the way in which, in the so-called 'classical' cinema, it is the system of representation itself which holds itself aloof, disconnects itself, takes itself apart, and thus renders its mechanisms legible without having to resort to so-called 'modern' rupturing effects, contradictions of pseudo-distantiation. Of how, in fact, the over-celebrated *transparency* was itself merely a snare, a preconceived idea.) On the other hand, this business of the reflected look is precisely what captures our own look and inscribes it in the mirror, superimposing it in the reflection on Gruber's look. The 'placing in the abyss' also places *us* in the abyss by including our view (also as a short-circuit) in the circulation of represented views. A pattern is established of which we, in our position as spectators, form part. Gruber sees himself seen — He sees himself — He sees himself see himself — We see him seen — We see him — We see him see himself — *We see ourselves see him.* And, one might venture to say, he sees us see him.

A third element is included both in Gruber's view and in our own: the reflection in the mirror of the fiancé's look. This whole system of interception and elucidation (implicate to explicate) is also reinforced by the choice of angles in shooting: the deep focus effects in the mirror and the effect of an oblique perspective show us that there is an occupied locus reflected in the mirror which is symmetrical to our own: that of the fiancé's look at Gruber, which Gruber sees and which makes his scrutiny (along with ours) turn on himself. The image, in fact, of a spectator like us, who nevertheless does not really represent us inasmuch as no process of identification has linked us to him: a spectator-function, rather, observing ours, since the incidence of the mirror and the reversibility of the perspective mean that this spectator-function could be watching us watching. Something has us in view in Gruber's scrutiny of these depths, and since his scrutiny has captured ours, we watch ourselves.

The result is that at the end of this crucial scene, which marks Gruber's arrival at the truth and his catching up with it, we again find ourselves a little more deeply involved in a *forced* identification with Gruber. It was his body, and not those of the heroes, which everything made us identify as positive. It was his resistance which the fiction made us share, and not the forward flight of the resistants themselves. And now we have reached the same point, we have coincided for the duration of a look. Forced identification, because of course we cannot accept it, because it repels us on principle, because it is ruled out by the 'Nazi' referent[16] and the hatred it invokes. This identification is therefore simultaneously imposed by the fictional system and rejected by the *proper place* that is programmed for us. It is difficult to stay there, in this place which changes place and veers in a direction which is not the right one, towards a position where something splits, where we are caught up in a conflict impossible to resolve. No longer the one explicitly formulated by the fiction — must the hostages be saved, and how? — but another, insidiously substituted for the first:[17] if we are indeed on the side of the resistants, what is this side, is it indeed *the other* to that of the hangmen?

16. The point, we said, was for these fictions to put an end to their referents. *Hangmen Also Die* simply liquidates Nazism as a historical reference the moment it puts us in this untenable position.

17. The stratagem does not serve simply to suppress an insoluble politico-moral debate, to leap over the propaganda film impasse: more insidiously, by reversing the relationship between the lines of force (1st movement: Nazism versus the resistance; 2nd movement: the resistance versus Nazism) while limiting itself to simply inverting the roles term for term, it induces us to welcome the suppression of the debate: instead of being divided between the good by the wicked, we are united with the good against the wicked; and together in paying the price for this vengeful pleasure, which is that ultimately, without being aware of it, we are made to cut across the debate by accepting here that the end justifies the means provided the cause is good.

Gruber's death makes this unease that is beginning to seize us even more evident. Now that he has understood, Gruber heads straight for the goal (for death). He calls unexpectedly on Dr Svoboda at the hospital where he works: in the very place, in other words, used by Svoboda to establish his alibi (at the time Heydrich was assassinated, he was operating on a patient there). Although well aware that he has been lied to all along the line and that the complicity between Svoboda and Mascha Novotny is something other than that between two lovers, Gruber (like ourselves) is as yet unable to shake this formidable alibi. He is not required to do so. He does not have to unmask Dr Svoboda, who does it himself. Dr Svoboda and his assistant are coming out of the operating theatre. Both are wearing white coats and both are masked. These two almost identical forms, these two *uniforms*, these duplicating masks produce an effect of perceptional confusion. Making the same mistake as we do, Gruber assumes the assistant to be the doctor, takes the fake for the real. Immediately Svoboda identifies himself, literally unmasks himself. And with Gruber, we understand: masked, one surgeon is much like another; a uniform can have as many doubles as you like. Far from resisting this interpretation, Svoboda tranquilly confirms it: there is no longer any need for deception since Gruber is condemned by his knowledge. More than ever, truth = death.

His execution in the surgeons' changing-room functions as a dual trap: for him, for us. For him, he is not confronted by one man (body) or even two, but by something monstrous, two parallel and identical masses which advance and converge on him like automata in motion (this is how it is shot),[18] two fixed dead stares riveted on him, *and which* (this is how it is shot) *his own eyes are unable to sustain simultaneously*. This is when he begins to panic, to realise that he has lost, in being constantly watched from the side he is not watching. In being unable to adjust simultaneously to these two images, to this duplicated image which has his own body as its point of convergence. In being transfixed from the side where his own eyes no longer defend him: where he is blind, where he is *already* killed. There is no sense of a duel, of defiance, of fight in this ineluctably controlled execution. Despite the (good) cause which justifies it, there is nothing heroic about it. Quite the contrary. The two figures of retribution are shown to us *as Gruber sees them*: two death machines, two sub-human mechanisms, two funeral agents of hatred. The trap therefore functions *for us as well*. Whatever hatred we may in

---

18. The lighting in the scene carries the same sense, intensifying the phantasmal aspect of the two identical doctors closing in on Gruber, sending the twin dark shadows of the two white masses out towards him. The effects of visual stylisation here reinforce the symbolic charge of the scene.

fact still feel for Gruber — certainly more for what he represents than for his character as represented — it is difficult to sustain any at this moment of his death, within this scheme where he not only occupies the place of the victim (which is well and good: some deserve their fate), but more particularly where the two executioners, the two resistants, are through a strange reversal of values unequivocally placed in the intolerable position of being 'the hangmen'.

While we see these two nightmare images from Gruber's point of view as they advance on him (on *us*, therefore), we also advance with them, at their pace, towards their (our) target. Rarely have reverse angle set-ups implied, as here, the effective yet impossible rending of the spectator, who is simultaneously trapped within both fields of vision. The camera is in fact placed behind the two killers, who advance from the edges of the frame to converge on the centre of the image (Gruber). We are in the direct line of this vanishing point, and our field of vision corresponds to the base of this triangle whose two lateral angles are the two 'doubles', and the apex, Gruber. This means that Gruber's position, in the axis of our vision, is symmetrical to ours. It also means that Gruber is up against a third viewpoint, an axial one: ours. With us already in a position homologous to that of the killers, whom we see from the back, facing Gruber together, a terrifying slow forward track makes us share even more in their movement. One view put us alongside Gruber; the reverse angle inexorably identifies us with his killers. And no more from this point of view than from the other can Gruber's death be felt as a victory for the just, or even greeted with relief as putting an end to the menace which threatened the heroes: we don't care too much about these heroes,[19] there is nothing particularly attractive about them except their cause; and at this point in the fiction, this cause is in any case beginning to turn sour on us.

The resistants are successful in their machination. We now see those same representatives of the people of Prague, those taxi-drivers, workmen and waiters whom we saw refusing to talk under Nazi questioning at Gestapo HQ, courageously resisting interrogation and torture, showing great dignity and determination in standing up to threats and violence in order to bury the secret of Heydrich's assassin beneath the solemnity of collective silence — we now see them coming of their own accord to the Gestapo and all telling the same story to these same Nazis before even being asked, chorusing evidence to point to one and the same 'culprit'. Of course they are only doing this on orders from the clandestine organisation. Of course it is a trap being set for the

---

19. The fiction itself is the first to acknowledge this by not even taking the trouble to unravel the situations it has created: we learn nothing of an eventual (?) reconciliation between Mascha Novotny and her fiancé, nothing about Professor Novotny, etc. Not that this matters, since we have invested so little concern in the characters.

Gestapo. But the effect of these contrary repetitions remains strange. What do we see? Opposite the barbarous and ultra-automated Nazi machine another machine is erected, no less ruthless and no less mechanical.

Objection may be made that the two are not comparable. Yet the way the fiction functions, notably in its repetition effects and its insistence on automatisms, suggests that they may be compared[20] and that they may in some way be equivalent. Automata on the one hand, automata on the other. Lessons parroted, mechanical diction, voices that ring untrue, manipulation of minds and bodies, ramification of the lie spread over the entire community, fabrication and accumulation of snares: the conspiracy by the resistants simultaneously reveals a military accent, a demand for absolute and passive obedience, a marked effect of depersonalisation in the conspirators, and a lethal inflexibility which ultimately hardly inspire confidence. One is amused to see the Gestapo so thoroughly gulled. One is amused to see the brewer Czaka, the perfect black sheep, capitalist and traitor, shattered by the anguish of being accused of the one thing of which he is not guilty. The amusement does not last very long. Unease begins to replace the sense of liberation. Although we are aware of Czaka's not inconsiderable guilt, and have witnessed his betrayal of the resistance, we also know, with absolute certainty, that he is innocent at least of the deed for which he is condemned. And once again, everything within the film's system urges us to think that it is probably *as much* for this tiny particle of innocence as for the sum of his faults that he must pay with his death. Just as everything in the representation of this death — on the square in front of a church — turns it into the consummation of a sort of martyr's progress. Stricken by the false testimony and stagecraft of the resistants, abandoned by his Nazi friends who are provisionally satisfied with the scapegoat offered to them, Czaka describes a twin trajectory,[21] in opposite directions, whose effects are registered on his body, one of the

20. Arguably the film itself makes this impossible, this scandalous comparison. The leader of the resistance dies of his wounds and our heroes are at his bedside. The lighting effects and music tell us that Assumption attends this death. Then comes an insert, to bizarre effect: the body of Heydrich embalmed in a chapel lit with tapers. Of course this sets one death alongside the other. But it also implies a logic of equivalence, of exchange: one against the other, one for the other, one like the other. Two leaders, two dead leaders, two funeral vigils: no matter how much we may prefer one, the other is there. Placed on the same level? Equality, identity in death? Or, perhaps, ideological opposition within an expressive confusion?

21. This is represented in the scene of Czaka's confrontation with his accusers on one hand, and on the other, his less and less dependable Nazi friends. Czaka goes from one to the other, approaching the group of restaurant employees leagued against him as though to attach himself to them, then returning to the desk with the Nazi inquisitors, without securing a purchase or support on either side.

only ones (along with Gruber's) which the fiction battens on to.[22] Downfall and degradation: from power, fortune and luxury to repudiation and insignificance; and, concurrently, ascension and martyrdom: from vanity, cowardice and dissolution to that sort of heroism of the outcast or the expiatory victim, to the madness which is both punishment and election. It is when Czaka no longer matters to anybody in the fiction that he begins to matter to us. As Gruber does because he accedes to the truth, so Czaka dies because he incarnates for himself alone (and for us) his own particular truth (he did not kill Heydrich) which the two opposing machines unite to deny. But unlike what happens with Gruber, the fictional scheme and system of representation have always kept Czaka severely distanced from us, obviating sympathy — identification even more so — and we too are therefore led, in line with the coalition of accusers, to condemn him ruthlessly.

To keep pace with the machines: is this what the film also condemns us to? Or is it only (but this is not exclusive) a matter, as in most of Lang's fictions, of *making the spectator pay for his place*? If the fiction makes death circulate among the characters, the fictional scheme which governs the spectator's place makes it a journey of *mortification*. All convictions are crushed and chastened, any enthusiasms punished: ideological or emotional adherence to 'good causes' along with desire for the truth, illusions about justice along with identifications, the impulses of the characters along with the spectator's voyeuristic impulse, which is subjected to snares, destined to blindness. The spectator here has not the slightest choice, any more than the characters have. There are no rules for the game, there is no game, unless it be Hobson's choice (offering, of course, no *good* alternative): there is, in other words, not the slightest gratification. The scheme takes pains to include the spectator *in the fiction*, so that if he espouses the characters' cause, he also shares their fate in being manoeuvred: a system of manipulation which has the arrogant honesty to admit that it is so. A fiction concerning hate, yes, but first and foremost hatred of the spectator.

(Translated by Tom Milne)

22. Strange that the only two characters whose deaths are represented with violence and intensity in the film should be those whose bodies figure so prominently, as though this must be paid for, having a body, by a more cruel and exorbitant death.

Conclusion

If final proof were needed that the Lang-text still needs to be freed from the (essentially two) conventional ways of fixing its meaning, then one need look no further than Richard Roud's *Cinema: A Critical Dictionary*. Placed back to back as alternative ways of reading the text are articles by Noël Burch and Robin Wood. For Burch, 'From 1920 to 1932, along with Eisenstein and Dreyer, Lang (1890–1976) was one of the principal architects of that *langage sans langue* . . . which, according to Christian Metz, is cinema. From 1933 onwards, exiled from Nazi Germany and settling shortly thereafter in the United States, he seemingly accepted all the (essentially regressive) inferences which the American sound film had drawn in particular from his best work in Germany; whether consciously or not he identified himself with that anonymous being who was always much of a muchness, the all-purpose Hollywood director . . . *M* is not merely superior to *Fury* but belongs to an altogether different dimension'. For Wood, the essential task is to account for the text in such a way that 'a coherent portrait of Lang as an artist begins to emerge'. The knowledge produced by this account is that 'The central characterising tension of Lang's cinema . . . is that between morality and fate'. In other words the choices of perspective have hardly changed. Admittedly Burch's anti-Hollywood position springs from his interest in 'radical' narrative strategies, rather than simple critical snobbery, and Wood inflects the 'Lang as fatalist' position with his particular obsession with an artist's moral sensibility. Otherwise . . .

In fact, Robin Wood's essay does, almost unwittingly, suggest a third perspective. The one point at which his eulogy starts to crack is when he confronts the notion of 'Lang's feminine ideal [which] is not likely to recommend itself in these days of Women's Liberation, and it would not be difficult to argue that it points to a retrograde element in Lang's work'. It is hoped that the later sections of this book indicate that what Wood is hinting at, and basically repressing (sexual difference, desire, the 'problem' of the female), can be of vital importance in rethinking the Lang-text, once the obsession with the director as coherent and laudable subject is abandoned. Other strategies remain to be explored: Bellour's suggestion about the problematic relationship of Lang's films to various genres, or the connections between the films and their production contexts (industrial rather than simply geographical). The use value of the Lang-text, as opposed to its frozen meaning, is only beginning to emerge.

STEPHEN JENKINS

Fritz Lang:
A Documentary Record

The following section consists of bio/biblio/filmo-graphical information, intended as a basic chart of the space marked by Lang's name. There are several quotations from Julian Petley (BFI Distribution Library Catalogue 1978), Lotte Eisner, Luc Moullet and Enno Patalas (from their various books entitled Fritz Lang*). Unless noted otherwise quotations ascribed to Lang are from the Peter Bogdanovich interview book* Fritz Lang in America. *The book by Patalas* et al. *contains detailed credits, and a great deal of additional bibliographical information.*

1890   Fritz Lang born in Vienna, 5 December. His father, Anton, an architect. Attended Volkschule, Realschule. Later studied architecture, following his father's wishes. Abandoned architecture after developing an interest in painting, which he also studied formally.

1911–12 Undertook extensive travels, as far afield as Russia, Asia Minor and North Africa.

1913   Lived in Paris, earning a living as an artist.

1914   With the outbreak of war, Lang returned to Vienna and enlisted.

1916   Wrote first scripts while in military hospital. It is not known if the first, *Peitsche*, was ever filmed.
Worked as a stage actor, and sold scripts to the Decla company.

1917   **Die Hochzeit in Ekzentrik Klub** (Ufa). Dir: Joe May. Sc: Lang.
Hilde Warren und der Tod (Ufa). Dir: Joe May. Sc: Lang, who also played four roles in the film.

1918   Worked as story editor for Erich Pommer, head of Decla-Film, in Berlin. Wrote scripts, acted in several films, was assistant director to Joe May on *Herrin der Welt* (1919).

1918–19   **Die Rache ist Mein** (Decla). Dir: Alwin Neuss. Sc: Lang.
Bettler GmbH (Decla). Dir: unknown. Sc: Lang.

1919   **Wolkenbau und Flimmerstern** (Decla). Dir: unknown. Sc: Lang.
Halbblut (Decla). Dir/Sc: Lang. Ph: Carl Hoffmann. With: Ressel Orla, Carl de Vogt, Gilda Langer.
Der Herr der Liebe (Decla-Helios). Dir: Lang. Sc: Leo Koffler. Ph: Emil Schünemann. With: Carl de Vogt, Gilda Langer.
Totentanz (Helios). Dir: Otto Rippert. Sc: Lang.
Die Frau mit den Orchideen (Decla). Dir: Otto Rippert. Sc: Lang.
Die Spinnen (Part 1: Der goldene See) (Decla). Dir/Sc: Lang. Ph: Emil Schünemann. Art dir: Hermann Warm, Otto Hunte, Carl Ludwig Kirmse, Heinrich Umlauff. With: Carl de Vogt *(Kay Hoog)*, Lil Dagover *(Priestess of the Sun)*, Ressel Orla *(Lio Sha)*, Georg John *(Dr Telphas)*, Paul Morgan *(Expert)*.

Lang spoke of the appeal of adventurous and exotic subjects which enabled him to make use of his memories of his pre-World War One travels.

In *From Caligari to Hitler*, Siegfried Kracauer ascribes the popularity of this kind of film ('sensational adventures encountered at every known or unknown spot on earth') in post-World War One Germany to the desire of the German people, trapped in their 'mutilated and blockaded fatherland', to re-annex the world, at least in their imagination. Lotte Eisner quotes the trade press of the time which characterises the film as an attempt to capture some of the market cornered by the American film industry and its Westerns, and she also describes how the imagery of the film both draws on other sources and prefigures elements which will occur in Lang's later work.

Pest in Florenz (Decla). Dir: Otto Rippert. Sc: Lang.
Hara-kiri (Decla). Dir:Lang. Sc: Max Jungk, from the play *Madam Butterfly* by John Luther Long, David Belasco. Ph: Max Fassbaender. Art dir: Heinrich Umlauff. With: Paul Biensfeldt *(Daimyo Tokiyawa)*, Lil Dagover *(O-Take San)*, Georg John *(Monk)*, Meinhard Maur *(Prince Matahari)*.

Lang was scheduled to direct *The Cabinet of Dr Caligari*, but Pommer was forced to take him off the project. The first part of *Die Spinnen* proved so successful that Part Two was needed immediately. The idea of the framing prologue and epilogue in *Caligari* was supposedly Lang's.

149

1920   **Die Spinnen (Part 2: Das Brillantenschiff)** (Decla). Credits as for Part 1, except, Ph: Karl Freund. With: Carl de Vogt (*Kay Hoog*), Ressel Orla (*Lio Sha*), Rudolf Lettinger (*John Terry*), Thea Zander (*Ellen Terry*).
Signed with Joe May Company as writer-director.
Das wandernde Bild (Joe May Company). Dir: Lang. Sc: Lang, Thea von Harbou. Ph: Guido Seeber. Art dir: Otto Hunte, Erich Kettelhut. With: Mia May *(Irmgard Vanderheit)*, Hans Marr *(Georg Vanderheit, John his brother)*, Rudolf Klein Rhoden *(Wil Brand, Georg's cousin)*.
Returned to work for Pommer and Decla, now Decla-Bioscop.
Married Thea von Harbou.

1920–21 **Die Vier um die Frau** (Decla-Bioscop). Dir: Lang. Sc: Lang, Von Harbou. Ph: Otto Kanturek. Art dir: Ernst Meiwers, Hans Jacoby. With: Carola Toelle *(Florence Yquem)*, Hermann Boettcher *(Her father)*, Ludwig Hartau *(Harry Yquem)*, Anton Edthofer *(Werner Krafft/William, his brother)*, Rudolf Klein-Rogge *(Upton)*.

1921 · **Der müde Tod** (Decla-Bioscop). Dir: Lang. Sc: Von Harbou. Ph: Eric Nitzschmann, Hermann Saalfrank, Fritz Arno Wagner. Art dir: Robert Herlth, Walter Röhrig, Hermann Warm. With: Lil Dagover *(The Girl)*, Walter Janssen *(Her Lover)*, Bernhard Goetzke *(Death)*, Rudolf Klein-Rogge, Georg John.

In his article 'Happily Ever After?' (*Penguin Film Review* no. 5, 1948), Lang describes the cultural atmosphere of post-World War One Europe and America as one of 'pessimistic outcry. All over the world, young people engaged in the cultural fields, myself among them, made a fetish of tragedy. . . swinging from naive nineteenth-century sweetness and light to the opposite extreme of pessimism for its own sake'.
Julian Petley relates the film to Lang's general obsession with Fate in its various guises and points out that this obsession is expressed as much through Lang's *mise en scène* as it is through plot. He suggests that while the film relates in some ways to Expressionist concerns, it draws more upon the world of German Romanticism (death, alchemy, fairy tale figures, the supernatural) and authors like Hölderlin, Novalis, Tiech, the Brothers Grimm and Hoffmann.

Das indische Grabmal (Joe May Company). Dir: Joe May. Sc: Lang, Von Harbou.

1921–22 **Dr Mabuse der Spieler (Part 1: Der grosse Spieler—ein Bild der Zeit; Part 2: Inferno, ein Spiel von Menschen unserer Zeit)** (Uco-film). Dir: Lang. Sc: Lang, Von Harbou, from Norbert Jacques' novel. Ph: Carl Hoffmann. Art dir: Carl Starl-Urach, Otto Hunte, Erich Kettelhut, Karl Vollbrecht. With: Rudolf Klein-Rogge *(Dr Mabuse)*, Aud Egede Nissen *(Cara Carozza)*, Gertrude Weckler *(Countess Told)*, Alfred Abel *(Count Told)*, Bernhard Goetzke *(Wenk)*, Paul Richter *(Hull)*.

Julian Petley points to the suitability of the thriller genre as a vehicle for Lang's world view — 'a world in which nothing is as it seems, where danger lurks beneath the most normal seeming circumstances and objects, and individual destinies are threatened by mysterious and powerful forces... This is an early demonstration of a key Langian theme: the complete unreliability of appearances.'

Luc Moullet, on the other hand, describes the film as a 'phenomenological study' of 'the gestures and attitudes of human beings... which owes everything to improvisation and almost nothing to expressionism, and which strongly resembles modern cinema, in particular recent works by Lang, such as *Human Desire*'. The value of the film lies in its objectivity.

Lotte Eisner relates the decor of the film to movements in design other than Expressionism, such as the Viennese secession and Art Deco.

1922–24 **Die Nibelungen (Part 1: Siegfried; Part 2: Kriemhilds Rache)** (Decla-Bioscop-Ufa). Dir: Lang. Sc: Von Harbou. Ph: Carl Hoffmann, Günther Rittau; for 'Dream of the Falcon' sequence, Walter Ruttmann. Art dir: Otto Hunte, Erich Kettelhut, Karl Vollbrecht. With: Paul Richter *(Siegfried)*, Margaret Schön *(Kriemhild)*, Rudolf Klein-Rogge *(Etzel, King of the Huns)*, Georg August Koch *(Hildebrand)*, Theodor Loos *(Gunther)*, Bernhard Goetzke *(Volker von Alzey)*.

'Part Two is dialectically opposed to Part One. If *Siegfried* concerns the working out of Destiny through the rites and rituals of an authoritarian society set in a hostile and domineering landscape, then *Kriemhilds Rache* shows how Destiny can work itself out through the destructive unleashing of human passions. Revenge and the destructive forces of the psyche are key themes in Lang's oeuvre and find one of their strongest and most pessimistic expressions here. Lang's shift of focus is reflected in his *mise en scène*: the static architecturalism of the first part here gives way to a dynamic, even delirious

151

sense of movement. The actors are no longer slaves to or components of the decor, and are allowed far freer rein in this respect; however, they are now slaves to their own uncontrollable impulses.' (Julian Petley)

1924 Lang visited New York and Hollywood to study film production.

1925–6 **Metropolis** (Ufa). Dir: Lang. Sc: Lang, Von Harbou. Ph: Karl Freund, Günther Rittau. Art dir: Otto Hunte, Erich Kettelhut, Karl Vollbrecht. Special Effects: Eugen Schüfftan. With: Alfred Abel *(Fredersen)*, Gustav Fröhlich *(Freder)*, Rudolf Klein-Rogge *(Rotwang)*, Brigitte Helm *(Maria)*.

In connection with this film Julian Petley mentions Oswald Spengler's *Decline of the West* and the 'strong current of . . . agrarian mysticism running through much German thought', and quotes Spengler's description of the city as 'a daemonic stone desert', 'an artificial, mathematical, utterly land-alien product of a pure intellectual satisfaction'.

Lotte Eisner relates Lang's handling of crowd scenes to the influence of the stage director Erwin Piscator: 'the *Ballung* (agglomeration of human figures) of the *Sprechchore* (speaking chorus). . . In the *Sprechchore* the crowd became a compact sombre mass, often almost amorphous, subject to a heavy machine-like movement from which, at rhythmic intervals, a single character, a leader of the chorus, detached himself. For Piscator, who was greatly influenced by Russian stage production, the Expressionist anonymous man belonged to a collectivity, and his body expressed either forward-bounding or restrained Will. . . He even contrived to transform extras into architectural elements.'

1927 **Spione** (Ufa). Dir/Prod: Lang. Sc: Lang, Von Harbou. Ph: Fritz Arno Wagner. Art dir: Otto Hunte, Karl Vollbrecht. With: Rudolf Klein-Rogge *(Haighi)*, Gerda Maurus *(Sonja)*, Lien Deyers *(Kitty)*, Craighall Sherry *(Burton Jason)*, Willy Fritsch *(Tremaine)*, Lupu Pick *(Masimoto)*.

Luc Moullet and Jonathan Rosenbaum, the latter in his *Monthly Film Bulletin* review (May 1976), comment on the film's elaborate plotting. Moullet sees it as 'a web of actions and motivations, too numerous and too cursorily presented, which corresponds to that which governs our lives', i.e. a further manifestation of the web of Destiny in which man is trapped. Rosenbaum reads the découpage as a 'brilliant forecast . . . of *M* (which links together alien social patterns in a montage pattern structured round a central figure who goads these forces into action and eventually becomes their victim). . . On a more strictly formal level, the remarkably elliptical editing . . . contrives to organise the extraordinary density of the overlapping intrigues into a lucid pattern that has served as a sourcebook and object lesson for many subsequent master plotters, from Hitchcock and Graham Greene to Rivette, Straub and Thomas Pynchon'.

1928–29   **Frau im Mond** (Ufa). Dir/Prod: Lang. Sc: Von Harbou, based on her novel. Ph: Curt Courant, Oskar Fischinger, Otto Kanturek. Art dir: Otto Hunte, Emil Hasler, Karl Vollbrecht. With: Gerda Maurus *(Frieda Venten)*, Willy Fritsch *(Prof. Helius)*, Fritz Rasp *(Walt Turner)*, Klaus Pohl *(Prof. Manfeldt)*, Gustav von Wangenheim *(Hans Windegger)*.

Barthelemy Amengual in *Cahiers de la Cinémathèque*, no. 12, has described this film as 'the perfect example of those works in which the auteur theory imposes its legitimacy' precisely because the 'Langian presence' is heard 'in a minor key'. Lang the architect and the organiser of crowds can be seen in the design of the rocket hangar and the scene of the lift-off. 'The expressionist of *Mabuse* also conceived of these mad scientists, financial sharks, demons of the will to power, who are spreading the darkness of the industrial capitalist world.' Amengual predictably continues that 'the clearest indication of the Langian presence is attached to the figure of Destiny', manifested here, as always with Lang, externally, in the design of the rocket, 'which is as partitioned off and discontinuous as a prison'. The only defence erected against Destiny, as in *Fury*, *You Only Live Once* and *You and Me*, is the unity of the couple, established here when Frieda, who has hidden herself outside the rocket, reappears after it has left for earth, abandoning her lover, whom she rejoins.

1931   **M** (Nero Film). Prod: Seymour Nebenzal. Dir: Lang. Sc: Lang, Von Harbou. Ph: Fritz Arno Wagner. Sound Editor: Paul Falkenberg. Art dir: Emil Hasler, Karl Vollbrecht. With: Peter Lorre *(Hans Beckert)*, Ellen Widmann *(Frau Beckmann)*, Gustav Gründgens *(Schränker)*, Otto Wernicke *(Lohmann)*.

To a greater extent than any other of Lang's films, *M* has been accorded 'classic' status in almost all versions of the history of the cinema. In an article entitled 'De Mabuse à M: le Travail de Fritz Lang' (published in the collection of essays *Cinéma:*

Théories, Lectures, Textes, edited by Dominique Noguez, 1973), Noël Burch has adopted a position consciously contrary to that of the *Cahiers* critics. Consigning Lang's American films to the anonymous body of work which, he thinks, constitutes the narrative cinema of that country, a cinema of transparency, he argues that certain of Lang's German films, particularly *M,* mark crucial points in the development of film narrative. The first *Mabuse,* in his view, shows a perfect mastery of that narrative code based on the maintenance of the illusion of continuity, maintained to the extent that an awareness of shot changes is rendered almost occult, despite the fact that the film of necessity proceeds by découpage. At the same time, however, Lang works on the breaks between scenes, exploiting the dialectical possibilities of the introduction of an element of discontinuity at the heart of the film's narrative continuity. *M* furthers this work. Burch divides the film into nine sections, each with its own mode of functioning, but with certain main controlling principles in the film as a whole. Two large movements pervade it, one from the discontinuous towards the continuous, in terms of the découpage, the other the gradual unveiling of the murderer. The work thus assumes unity but tends towards diversity, since the structures of the film can be read in the abstract, while being in 'symbiosis with the plot, of which they are at once the support and the denunciator'. Burch's work on 'Codes in crisis' is developed in an article (written with Jorge Dana) in *Afterimage* no. 5, entitled 'Propositions'.

1932   **Das Testament des Dr Mabuse** (Nero Film). Dir/Prod: Lang. Sc: Von Harbou. Ph: Fritz Arno Wagner, Karl Vash. Art dir: Karl Vollbrecht, Emil Hasler. Mus: Hans Erdmann. With: Rudolf Klein-Rogge *(Mabuse),* Oskar Beregi *(Dr Baum),* Otto Wernicke *(Lohmann),* Wera Liessem *(Lilli),* Gustav Diessl *(Kent).* A French version was shot simultaneously with the German.

This film was banned by the Nazis in 1933, according to *Kinematograph,* 'for legal reasons . . . of endangering public order and security'. Goebbels has been quoted as saying, 'I shall ban the film . . . because it proves that a group of men who are determined to the last . . . could succeed in overturning any government by brute force'.
Lang stated his intention thus: 'This film showed Hitler's terror methods as in a parable. The slogans and beliefs of the Third Reich were placed in the mouths of criminals. By these

means I hoped to expose those doctrines behind which there lurked the intention to destroy everything a people holds dear.' (Quoted by Lotte Eisner)

1933–34 **Liliom** (S.A.F.-Fox Europa). Dir: Lang. Prod: Erich Pommer. Sc: Lang, Robert Liebmann, Bernard Zimmer. Based on Ferenc Molnar's play. Ph: Rudolf Maté, Louis Née. Mus: Jean Lenoir, Franz Waxman. Art dir: Paul Colin, René Renoux. Asst. dir: Jacques Feydeau. With: Charles Boyer *(Liliom)*, Madeleine Ozeray *(Julie)*, Florelle *(Mme Muskat)*, Robert Arnoux *(Strong Arm)*, Antonin Artaud *(Knife-grinder)*.

Lang fled from Germany after Goebbels offered him the leading post in the German film industry. According to Lang, despite the banning of *Testament of Dr Mabuse*, Hitler had been very impressed by *Metropolis*, and considered Lang the right person to make national socialist films.
When Lang arrived in Paris he met Erich Pommer, who was there representing the French branch of Fox (having himself fled from the Nazis), and for Fox he made *Liliom*.
The film is interesting for the replaying of sections of Liliom's life on a kind of celestial television, an early instance in Lang's work of the introduction of a system of representation into the film text itself. Luc Moullet has pointed out that this is not an hommage to his art, but rather a critique of 'the uncertainty of objectivity . . . appearances such as they are disclosed to us in the cinema are deceptive, and can easily be contradicted by the evidence of another moment, or of another shot from a different point of view'.
Molnar's play has also formed the basis of films by Borzage, in 1930; and by Henry King, who in 1956 filmed it as the musical *Carousel*.

1934 In London, Lang signed a contract with David Selznick to make one film for MGM, with an option on others. Moved to California.

1935 Became American citizen.

1935–36 **Fury** (MGM). Prod. Joseph Mankiewicz. Dir: Lang. Sc: Lang, Bartlett Cormack, from story by Norman Krasna. Ph: Joseph Ruttenberg. Art dir: Cedric Gibbons. Mus: Franz Waxman. With: Spencer Tracy *(Joe Wilson)*, Sylvia Sidney *(Katherine Grant)*, Walter Abel *(District Attorney)*, Bruce Cabot *(Kirby Dawson)*, Edward Ellis *(Sheriff)*.

Bernard Cohn *(Positif,* February 1964) suggests that 'It would be . . . a misconception to consider *Fury* as a film inscribed in the context of the American social cinema of the years 1935–40 *(Modern Times, Grapes of Wrath).* Lang does not give the phenomenon of lynching any social foundation. On the contrary, he shows the two main characters finding work with relative ease, which excludes . . . any reference to a rather intense state of crisis'. Lynching is a 'collective neurosis', the result of the pressure of subconscious forces on the individual, a displaced sexual hysteria. The film also exemplifies Lang's sense of determinism: 'Each object, each mark that a person leaves on his way, is indelible: the peanuts, the ring, even the slip which makes Joe say and write "momentum" instead of "memento", the newsreel.'

Cohn also points to the unbridgeable gap established between Joe Wilson's inner desire for revenge, and the 'truth' established by the process of the trial. Wilson can reconcile himself with the law only by standing apart from it: 'Something in me is shattered: faith in justice and in man.'

1936   **You Only Live Once** (Walter Wanger-United Artists). Dir: Lang. Prod: Walter Wanger. Sc: Gene Towne, Graham Baker. Ph: Leon Shamroy. Art dir: Alexander Tobuloff. Mus: Alfred Newman. With: Sylvia Sidney *(Joan Graham),* Henry Fonda *(Eddie Taylor),* Barton Maclane *(Stephen Whitney),* Jean Dixon *(Bonnie),* William Gargan *(Father Dolan).*

Gavin Lambert *(Sight and Sound,* Summer 1955) links the mood of *You Only Live Once* (and *You and Me*) to films made contemporaneously by Carné and Prévert such as *Quai des Brumes* and *Le Jour se lève,* rather than to what he calls 'the American social cinema of the Thirties' — this is in terms of both content ('the worker-hero rejected and penalised by society, the girl who identifies herself with his plight, their attempts to find happiness together frustrated by poverty and an inescapable past') and the common schematic structures of the films.

Jean Douchet *(Cahiers du Cinéma,* March 1958) reads the film in spiritual/mystical terms centring on the idea of Man wandering in a world 'forever deprived of the true light, the memory of which torments him. Desperately but in vain he tries to pierce the opaque shell in order to find again the light to which he aspires; he refuses to accept the curse, which makes of him a prisoner eternally condemned to death'. The imagery is that of an 'eternal fog . . . a closed universe (. . . fog, tear gas, misted over windows, rain . . .)'. Lang 'directs like a spider weaves his web: everything is implication. One image — where each element is situated in a place predetermined from the start — determines the next . . . The accusation of implausibility, so often advanced against Fritz Lang, therefore seems to me to be deprived of all foundation. How could there be implausibility since nothing occurs which could not be deduced from a preceding factor?'

Lang involved in the formation of the Hollywood Anti-Nazi League.

1937   Article by Georges Franju, 'Le Style de Fritz Lang', published in the magazine *Cinématographe* no. 3.

1938   **You and Me** (Paramount). Dir/Prod: Lang. Sc: Virginia Van Upp, from a story by Norman Krasna. Ph: Charles Lang Jr. Art dir: Hans Dreier, Ernest Fegté. Mus: Kurt Weill, Boris Morros. With: Sylvia Sidney *(Helen Roberts)*, George Raft *(Joe Dennis)*, Robert Cummings *(Jim)*, Barton Maclane *(Mickey)*, Harry Carey *(Mr Morris)*.

Lang told Peter Bogdanovich that, although he did not work on the script, 'there's no question that Brecht was most responsible for *You and Me* . . . In my opinion, Brecht is, up to now, the greatest talent of this century in Germany. He invented the epic theatre and something else — *Lehrstuck* — a play that teaches something . . . And I wanted to make a picture that teaches something in an entertaining way, with songs . . . But *You and Me* was an unfortunate affair from the beginning — you know, sometimes things are jinxed. In the middle of the picture [Kurt] Weill left — he didn't want to stay any longer, so he went to New York. It was very unfortunate'.

Enno Patalas, while admitting that Norman Krasna's story would have better suited a Capra 'fantasy of goodwill', sees Brecht's influence in the opening sequence ('You Can't Get Something for Nothing') and in the convicts' Christmas Eve reunion, which evolves into a reminiscence of life behind bars, an 'insert in the style of *The Threepenny Opera*'.

1940   **The Return of Frank James** (20th Century-Fox). Prod: Darryl F. Zanuck. Dir: Lang. Sc: Sam Hellman. Ph: George Barnes, William V. Skall (Technicolor). Art dir: Wiard B. Ihnen, Richard Day. Mus: David Buttolph. With: Henry

Fonda *(Frank James)*, Gene Tierney *(Eleanor Stone)*, Jackie Cooper *(Clem)*, Henry Hull *(Major Todd)*, John Carradine *(Bob Ford)*.

'It was an assignment, but I was interested . . . the Western is not only the history of this country, it is what the saga of the Nibelungen is for the European. I think the development of this country is unimaginable without the days of the Wild West.' (Lang)
Lang spoke of *Western Union* in similar terms: 'I don't think this picture really depicted the West as it *was*; maybe it lived up to certain dreams, illusions — what the Old Timers *wanted* to remember of the Old West.'

The title not only refers back to Henry King's *Jesse James* (1939), to which the Lang film was a follow-up, but also to the moral status of Frank James' revenge. 'Like the hero of *Fury*, Frank has the best reasons in the world for avenging his brother, but [owing to his moral integrity] . . . the law will have to prove itself unfit before he will pursue the Ford Brothers . . . Finally, returning home, vengeance accomplished, he can say: "Today I can look at myself in a mirror without blushing". . . Frank James becomes a moral example. He pursues a mode of behaviour which owes everything to personal reflection, and nothing to external temptations of legal solace or ideas of personal rebellion.' (Luc Moullet)

Western Union (20th Century-Fox). Dir: Lang. Sc: Robert Carson, from novel by Zane Grey. Ph: Edward Cronjager, Allen M. Davey (Technicolor). Art dir: Richard Day, Wiard B. Ihnen. Mus: David Buttolph. With: Robert Young *(Richard Blake)*, Randolph Scott *(Vance Shaw)*, Dean Jagger *(Edward Creighton)*, Virginia Gilmore *(Sue Creighton)*, Barton Maclane *(Jack Slade)*, John Carradine *(Doc Murdoch)*.

'In [Lang's] Westerns the *mise en scène* is simple, it suffices to serve the plot . . . the discretion and the rarity of the camera movements, the sobriety of the acting, American and classical, make for very austere works, even down to the choice of landscapes, which are a little too bleak. In the living universe of the Western they jar, almost annoyingly. It's true that this sobriety emphasises remarkably the moral dignity of the heroes, which is very well rendered by the cold concentration the actors bring to the parts. This lyrical rigour reminds one of Hawks, minus the humour.' (Luc Moullet)
Lang speaks of camera movement in terms of the repression of

'style' as such from the text: 'I honestly believe that any camera movement must have a reason. In my opinion, to move a camera just to move it is wrong. Camera movement must express something . . . only if you follow something that moves will the audience not notice the camera movement.'
Enno Patalas mentions the shot of the prairie seen through the land surveyor's device: 'Here the prairie appears not as the promised land of freedom, of unknown hope or danger, as with Ford or Vidor and other American-born authors, but from the perspective of a man with a goal, a builder. That the look of a deadly marksman is also fixed in the same way is not surprising with Lang, for whom building and destruction are inseparable. Utopia means as little in his Westerns as in his science fiction . . .'

Man Hunt (20th Century-Fox). Dir: Lang. Sc: Dudley Nichols, from novel *Rogue Male* by Geoffrey Household. Ph: Arthur Miller. Art dir: Richard Day, Wiard B. Ihnen. Mus: Alfred Newman. With: Walter Pidgeon (*Thorndike*), Joan Bennett (*Jenny*), George Sanders (*Quive-Smith*), John Carradine (*Mr Jones*), Roddy McDowell (*Vaner*).

Lang shot the scene of Joan Bennett and Walter Pidgeon's parting on London Bridge against Zanuck's orders. The latter did not consider tragic 'a whore playing a whore in front of the man she loves'. The fact that the scene is highly stylised was, according to Lang's account, more a matter of constraint than artistic intention: 'All we had were cobblestones on the street. Then I said "Ben (unit manager), I saw a railing around here that looks like a bridge." He said, "No, *that* you can have." But we needed two so I said, "How much would it cost to make a second one – at my expense?" I think it was forty dollars. I talked with Arthur Miller — he was a genius as a cameraman — and he said it was possible to light in such a way that the background gradually faded away in the fog. So we didn't even need a backdrop. We had the cobblestone street, and we had the sidewalk, on which we put those two railings. We had a lamp-post, and we hung progressively diminishing light-bulbs — say a hundred watt, then eighty, then fifty and so on; and over the whole thing we put a little London fog. We started at four o'clock in the morning . . . we were ready to shoot at eight o'clock.'
A three-part article by Otis Ferguson on Lang appeared in the *New Republic*. Lang worked ('I directed practically nothing') on *Confirm or Deny* (20th Century-Fox, Dir: Archie Mayo).

1942   Lang worked for four days on *Moontide* (20th Century-Fox, Dir: Archie Mayo).

Hangmen Also Die! (Arnold Productions-United Artists). Dir/Prod: Lang. Sc: Lang, Bertolt Brecht, John Wexley, from a story by Lang and Brecht. Ph: James Wong Howe. Art dir: William Darling. Mus: Hanns Eisler. With: Brian Donlevy *(Svoboda)*, Anna Lee *(Mascha Novotny)*, Walter Brennan *(Prof. Novotny)*, Gene Lockhart *(Emil Czaka)*, Alexander Granach *(Gruber)*.

Brecht's troubled involvement with the film is described in some detail by Lotte Eisner. The reader is also referred to Ben Brewster's article 'Brecht and the Film Industry' *(Screen*, vol. 16, no. 4, Winter 1975-76).
Enno Patalas relates the Brian Donlevy character to 'the hunted men in other Lang films. Except that he has "the people" on his side'. The image of the people has two faces — the sympathisers who relate to the 'spontaneously solid lynch mobs of *M* and *Fury*' and the 'conspiratorial group of activists' who spring from the criminal organisations controlled by Mabuse and Haighi. Patalas also points out that 'Lang even outwitted the Hays office. "It's against all my principles," said its chief, Joe Breen, "it is a glorification of lies, but I know that I cannot forbid it".'

1944   **The Ministry of Fear** (Paramount). Dir: Lang. Prod/Sc: Seton Miller, from Graham Greene's novel. Ph: Henry Sharp. Art dir: Hans Dreier, Hal Pereira. Mus: Victor Young. With: Ray Milland *(Stephen Neale)*, Marjorie Reynolds *(Carla Hilfe)*, Dan Duryea *(Travers)*, Carl Esmond *(Willi Hilfe)*, Hillary Brooke *(Mrs Bellane)*, Percy Waram *(Inspector Prentice)*.

Gavin Lambert *(Sight and Sound*, Autumn 1955) criticised *Ministry of Fear* and *Man Hunt* for being 'wrongly paced — too applied, too expository — and their (mainly nocturnal) London backgrounds are as weirdly synthetic as Pabst's in *Die Dreigroschenoper*'. By being 'overladen with suggestions of vague terror and menace in everything — a tree or a clock, even, seems macabre, a phenomenon or object of intrinsic ill-will — these films dissipate their real source of tension, the game of hunter and hunted'.
But Enno Patalas sees 'the isolation of objects and images in the time and space of a film' as, exactly, 'the poetic centre of Lang's films'. *The Ministry of Fear* provides him with the perfect opportunity to present 'everything in a surprising, ambiguous, unsettling light . . . Reality comes across to Ray Milland as the

insane imaginings of a madman, which is only, after all, what he had passed himself off as. It's as if his own lie would overtake him . . . with Lang, events and objects present contradictory, often deceptive, aspects'. And David Thomson *(Sight and Sound,* Spring 1977) describes how 'He [Lang] never relents from the exposition of significant action through space, shape and light: a designed image taut with irrational anxiety. If only to illustrate the order and consistency of his direction, notice the use of doorways and entrances in *The Ministry of Fear* . . . They connect spatial areas, serve as metaphors for progress and ordeal, comprise a visual pattern that neatly rhymes as the film progresses, so that the crazy adventure seems more than ever ordained.'

The Woman in the Window (Christie Corp.-International Pictures-RKO Radio). Dir: Lang. Prod/Sc: Nunnally Johnson, from novel *Once Off Guard* by J. H. Wallis. Ph: Milton Krasner. Art dir: Duncan Cramer. Mus: Arthur Lang. With: Edward G. Robinson *(Wanley),* Joan Bennett *(Alice),* Raymond Massey *(Lalor),* Dan Duryea *(Heidt),* Edward Breon *(Barkstone).*

Luc Moullet describes *Woman in the Window, Scarlet Street* and *Secret Beyond the Door* as a trilogy, 'to which one can add *House by the River,* and which can be defined as psychological, or rather psychoanalytic, criminal melodramas. After the struggle against Nazism, here is the struggle against oneself . . .'
In Wallis' novel, Wanley is a professor of literature not psychology, and the dream structure is absent. Lang's film thus foregrounds the notion of the Professor's experience as the eruption of repressed desire.
Lang claims ('Happily Ever After?', *Penguin Film Review* no. 5) that: 'If I had continued the story to its logical conclusion, a man would have been caught and executed for committing a murder because he was one moment off guard . . . I rejected this logical ending because it seemed to me a defeatist ending, a tragedy brought about by an implacable Fate.' But the film text as a whole ends with repression — Wanley this time rejects the advances of the female who accosts him. Which, coupled with the dream stylisation of the framed narrative (discussed by Alfred Appel Jr. in *Film Comment,* November 1974), suggests that Lang himself is repressing the implications of the text. This impression is strengthened by his assertion that 'I am not always objective about my own work, but in this case my choice was conscious'.

Diana Productions, an independent production company, formed. Lang was President, Walter Wanger Executive Vice-President.

Scarlet Street (Diana Productions-Universal). Dir/Prod: Lang. Sc: Dudley Nichols, from novel *La Chienne* by Georges de la Fouchardière. Ph: Milton Krasner. Art dir: Alexander Golitzen. Music: Hans J. Salter. With: Edward G. Robinson *(Chris Cross)*, Joan Bennett *(Kitty)*, Dan Duryea *(Johnny)*, Rosalind Ivan *(Adele)*, Jess Barker *(Janeway)*, Russell Hicks *(Hogarth)*.

Lang: 'The original idea was a film by Jean Renoir called *La Chienne*; naturally here it's impossible to call a picture *The Bitch*. Anyway Lubitsch very much wanted to make this picture in America, so Paramount bought it for him and he and two other men tried to adapt it but could never get a script . . . The Renoir film really is a wonderful picture but Nichols and I purposely never looked at it.' Gavin Lambert *(Sight and Sound*, Autumn 1955) described the film as 'finally only an exercise in low-life' because 'unlike Zola (in *Thérèse Raquin*) he [Lang] watches his dreadful lovers from outside; unlike Von Sternberg (in *The Blue Angel*) he does not create an atmosphere that acutely reflects the climate of its country and period'. Lambert's remarks 'acutely reflect' the British critical establishment's failure to deal constructively with films which 'failed' with regard to their fetish for naturalism, and which treated characters as functions from which the spectator is deliberately distanced.

An Index to the Creative Work of Fritz Lang by Herman Weinberg published as Special Supplement to *Sight and Sound*.

Cloak and Dagger (United States Pictures-Warner Bros.). Prod: Milton Sperling. Dir: Lang. Sc: Albert Maltz, Ring Lardner Jr. Ph: Sol Polito. Art dir: Max Parker. Mus: Max Steiner. Editor: Christian Nyby. With: Gary Cooper *(Alvah Jasper)*, Lilli Palmer *(Gina)*, Robert Alda *(Pinky)*, Vladimir Sokoloff *(Dr Polda)*, J. Edward Bronberg *(Trenk)*.

Warner Bros. cut and destroyed the entire last reel of the film, 'a warning against the new-born terror of the spread of the destructive capabilities of atomic power . . . Lang's central purpose in making the film' (Lotte Eisner). Why was it cut? 'You must ask Warners. I don't know. Maybe because it was after Hiroshima and Nagasaki.' (Lang)
'. . . Let's talk about Gary Cooper; he has his limitations, right?

To cast him as a top scientist is already unusual . . . I am
casting against image which I like to do . . . you cannot destroy
an actor by taking away his so-called personality. You have to
use him, but you try *slightly* to change some things . . .' (Lang)
'It's not surprising that Lang prefers to choose expressionless
actors as heroes . . . Man triumphs over adversity thanks to an
active patience, a stoicism which necessitates this mummified
acting, disliked by the critics.' (Luc Moullet)
'The opposite of a James Bond, Gary Cooper stumbles
through a hostile world. To be a secret agent was an old wish of
his . . . The childhood dream turns into a nightmare . . . like
most of Lang's heroes he is a rather contemplative type.'
(Enno Patalas)

1947   Article on Lang's style by Lotte Eisner published in *Revue du
Cinéma* no. 5.
Siegfried Kracauer's book *From Caligari to Hitler* is published,
containing writings on Lang's German films.
Article on Lang published in *Film Quarterly*.

Secret Beyond the Door (Diana Productions-Universal
International). Dir/Prod: Lang. Sc: Silvia Richards, from
novel *Museum Piece Number 13* by Rufus King. Ph: Stanley
Cortez. Art dir: Max Parker. Mus: Miklos Rozsa. With: Joan
Bennett *(Celia)*, Michael Redgrave *(Mark)*, Anne Revere
(Carrie), Barbara O'Neil *(Miss Robey)*, Paul Kavanagh *(Rick)*,
Mark Dennis *(David)*.

Lang claims Hitchcock's *Rebecca* as the direct inspiration for
this film: 'I'll tell you what the whole idea was. You remember
that wonderful scene in *Rebecca* where Judith Anderson talks
about Rebecca and shows Joan Fontaine the clothes and fur
coats and everything? . . . Talk about stealing — I had the
feeling that maybe I could do something similar in this picture
when Redgrave talks about the different rooms. Now let's be
very frank — it just didn't come through for me.'
But Gérard Legrand *(Positif,* April 1968) suggests that the
least productive way to read the film is to compare it with
Rebecca and 'the psychoanalytic films (e.g., *Spellbound)* which
Hitchcock was directing at the time'. The crucial difference is
Lang's avoidance of the use of symbolic and metaphorical
imagery. Legrand mentions the shot in *Spellbound* where
'Gregory Peck kisses Ingrid Bergman, and suddenly, in her
mind, a succession of doors opening, opening, opening to
infinity, towards the back of the image . . . It is at once love and
the presentiment of a formidable enigma, in a symbolic form.

Nothing like this in Lang: the doors which open and close here are not metaphors. One would look in vain for a symbol in this film: the sprig of lilacs which revives a fatal memory for the hero is still only lilacs'.

1948   Article by Lang, 'Happily Ever After?', published in *Penguin Film Review* no. 5. Article by Lotte Eisner, 'The German Films of Fritz Lang', published in *Penguin Film Review* no. 6.

1949   **House by the River** (Fidelity Pictures-Republic). Dir: Lang. Prod: Howard Welsch. Sc: Mel Dinelli, from novel by A. P. Herbert. Ph: Edward Cronjager. Art dir: Bert Leven. Mus: George Antheil. With: Louis Hayward *(Stephen Byrne)*, Lee Bowman *(John Byrne)*, Jane Wyatt *(Marjorie Byrne)*, Dorothy Patrick *(Emily Gaunt)*, Ann Shoemaker *(Mrs Ambrose)*.

The rarest Lang film still extant, *House by the River* is linked by Bertrand Tavernier *(Cahiers du Cinéma,* June 1962) to *Moonfleet* and *Rancho Notorious* in terms of their 'harrowing romanticism . . . across which Lang retains his lucid, critical gaze'. The Hayward character, whose murder of a servant girl becomes material for his novel, clearly points forward to Tom Garrett of *Beyond a Reasonable Doubt.* As Tavernier notes, 'Everything in this work is a sign of death', sign being the crucial term — totally 'unconvincing' sets, 'wooden' performances, characters suddenly appearing with the status of hallucination or memory, and the narrative content doubled by the discourse of the novel.

1950   **American Guerilla in the Philippines** (20th Century-Fox). Dir: Lang. Prod/Sc: Lamar Trotti, from novel by Ira Wolfert. Ph: Harry Jackson (Technicolor). Art dir: Lyle Wheeler, J. Russell Spencer. Mus: Cyril Mockridge. With: Tyrone Power *(Chuck Palmer)*, Micheline Presle *(Jeanne Martinez)*, Jack Elam *(Spenser)*, Bob Patten *(Lovejoy)*, Tom Ewell *(Mitchell)*.

'It was also offered to me — and even a director has to make a living! Honestly, I needed some money. Directors are often blamed: "Why did you do this? And why did you do that?" But nobody ever says "Even a director has to eat". Anyway we shot it all in the Philippines — the interiors too.' (Lang)
Lotte Eisner sees the film as thematically consistent with Lang's other war films: 'The basic situation is like those in *Man Hunt, Hangmen Also Die, Ministry of Fear* and *Cloak and Dagger.* The hero is suddenly in a situation where the enemy is everywhere. All activity is forced underground, all "normal"

activity becomes impossible. Slowly each character moves from passive action (escape, survival) to the more positive and active movement towards fighting back in the hope of final restoration of complete freedom of activity in a "normal" way.'

1951   Joseph Losey's remake of *M* (Superior Pictures-Columbia) is released.

Rancho Notorious (Fidelity Pictures-RKO Radio). Dir: Lang. Prod: Howard Welsch. Sc: Daniel Taradash, from a story by Silvia Richards. Ph: Hal Mohr (Technicolor). Art dir: Robert Priestley. Mus: Emil Newman. With: Marlene Dietrich *(Altar Keane)*, Arthur Kennedy *(Vern Haskell)*, Mel Ferrer *(Frenchy Fairmont)*, Gloria Henry *(Beth Forbes)*, William Frawley *(Baldy Gunder)*.

'Moral certainties and a peaceful life are torn apart at the beginning of the film, an average "normal" man is corrupted by hate, but nothing is restored to its former state by the end. The dark undertones of *The Return of Frank James* and *Western Union* have here come to the foreground; there will be no possibility of a return to the pastoral existence, no happy ending. Whatever redemption is possible for the characters is here only partial and carries the taste of "bitter and evil fruit" . . . It might even be argued that *Rancho Notorious* would not have worked half so well had it been shot on locations. The world of the film is a closed one, in which moral alternatives are limited, in which literally there is nowhere to go. The painted backdrops, beautiful in themselves, serve to emphasise the moral situation.' (Lotte Eisner)

1952   **Clash By Night** (Wald-Krasna Productions). Dir: Lang. Prod: Harriet Parsons. Sc: Alfred Hayes, from play by Clifford Odets. Ph: Nicholas Musuraca. Art dir: Albert D'Agostino, Jack Mills. Mus: Roy Webb. With: Barbara Stanwyck *(Mae Doyle)*, Paul Douglas *(Jerry D'Amato)*, Robert Ryan *(Earl Pfeiffer)*, Marilyn Monroe *(Peggy)*, J. Carroll Naish *(Uncle Vince)*, Paul Andes *(Joe Doyle)*.

'The problem in the picture was entirely different from the play, which was set against a social background of unemployment and so on, with a murder at the end: husband kills lover. The film was simply rewritten and edited by Alfred Hayes to give it a quite different aspect. I did a lot of research . . . about the faithfulness of wives. And I found in one of the leading women's magazines that 75 per cent of married women betray their husbands with extra-marital relationships. This became the problem in the film.' (Lang)

Nevertheless Enno Patalas suggests that the documentary-style introduction, shot on location, places the narrative in a material context of work and production, a little film about the journey made by fish, from being caught on the high seas to being tinned — a typical Langian mechanism.

The Barbara Stanwyck character can be compared to her similar roles in Douglas Sirk's *All I Desire* (1953) and *There's Always Tomorrow* (1955).

Lang experienced some difficulty in obtaining work after *Clash By Night*, which he ascribed to his having been placed on an anti-Communist blacklist.

1952–53 **The Blue Gardenia** (Blue Gardenia Productions-Gloria Films-Warner Bros). Dir: Lang. Prod: Alex Gottlieb. Sc: Charles Hoffmann, from a story by Vera Caspary. Ph: Nicholas Musuraca. Art dir: Daniel Hall. Mus: Raoul Kraushaar. With: Anne Baxter *(Norah)*, Richard Conte *(Casey Mayo)*, Ann Sothern *(Crystal)*, Raymond Burr *(Prebble)*, Jeff Donnell *(Sally)*.

When Bogdanovich suggested that the film was a 'venomous picture of American life', Lang replied: 'The only thing I can tell you about it is that it was the first picture after the McCarthy business and I had to shoot it in twenty days. Maybe that's what made me so venomous.'

But Eric Rohmer *(Cahiers du Cinéma,* June 1954) praises Lang for his 'objectivity vis à vis his characters', which he sees as 'far from the naturalism of the French school'. This objectivity is not 'as with a number of our other directors . . . just a corollary of impotence; if he does not like or exalt them [his characters] then he must scourge them, mercilessly'. For Rohmer, Lang's 'relish in the depiction of the situation of the three young American workers' was 'beating neo-realism on its own ground'.

1953 **The Big Heat** (Columbia). Dir: Lang. Prod: Robert Arthur. Sc: Sidney Boehm, from novel by William McGivern. Ph: Charles Lang Jr. Art dir: Robert Peterson. Mus: Daniele Amfitheatrof. With: Glenn Ford *(Dave Bannion)*, Gloria Grahame *(Debby Marsh)*, Jocelyn Brando *(Kate Bannion)*, Alexander Scourby *(Mike Lagana)*, Lee Marvin *(Vince Stone)*, Jeanette Nolan *(Bertha Duncan)*.

In her review in the *Monthly Film Bulletin* (April 1954), Penelope Houston could only set up an opposition between her idea of Lang as (fading) artist and her crude notion of genre. Thus 'in its *stereotyped* [my italics] way, the story of crime and administrative corruption is slickly written and directed, although Fritz Lang seems to have lost much of his old power to sustain dramatic tension'.

However, developments in film theory mean that the relationship between director/'artist' and genre cannot now be read as one of counterproductive opposition. Thus Colin McArthur in his book *Underworld USA* (1972) writes: 'It is a pity that Lang did not submit himself more frequently to the discipline of genre, for this discipline resulted in his most formally restrained and beautifully constructed film, *The Big Heat*, in which the narrative proceeds apace, but each scene is resonant with subtle, characteristically Langian meanings.' Dave Bannion's 'movement from policeman to avenger after the murder of his wife' makes him a typical Lang character, 'but Glenn Ford's grim unsmiling playing, and his brutal shape in battered hat and long trench coat are instantly expressive and typical of the genre'.

1954   Article, 'Aimer Fritz Lang', by François Truffaut, published in *Cahiers du Cinéma* (January)

Human Desire (Columbia). Dir: Fritz Lang. Prod: Lewis J. Rachmil. Sc: Alfred Hayes, from Zola's novel *La Bête Humaine*. Ph: Burnett Guffey. Art dir: Robert Peterson. Mus: Daniele Amfitheatrof. With: Glenn Ford *(Jeff Warren)*, Gloria Grahame *(Vicki Buckley)*, Broderick Crawford *(Carl Buckley)*, Edgar Buchanan *(Alec Simmons)*, Kathleen Case *(Ellen Simmons)*.

'Have you ever seen any other kind of desire? . . . Jerry Wald very much loved Renoir's picture *La Bête Humaine* (1938). Its hero was played by Jean Gabin, and he was a sex psychopath: he could only make love to a woman by killing her. Naturally in an American movie you cannot make the hero a sex killer . . . So Glenn Ford has to play it, you know, like Li'l Abner coming back from Korea — 100 per cent red-blooded American with very natural sex feelings (if such a thing exists).' (Lang)
Andrew Sarris *(Village Voice*, 7 December 1967) opposes Renoir's humanism to Lang's determinism, the former producing 'the tragedy of a doomed man caught up in the flow of life . . . the faces of Gabin, Simon and Ledoux', the latter 'the nightmare of an innocent man enmeshed in the tangled

strands of fate . . . geometrical patterns of trains, tracks, and camera angles'.

Philippe Demonsablon *(Cahiers du Cinéma,* August-September 1955) sees Broderick Crawford as the central character, his relationship with Gloria Grahame linking the film thematically to *Woman in the Window, Scarlet Street* and *Clash by Night,* 'the relations between a younger woman and an older man'.

1954–55 **Moonfleet** (MGM). Dir: Lang. Prod: John Houseman. Sc: Jan Lustig, Margaret Fitts, from novel by J. Meade Falkner. Ph: Robert Planck (Eastmancolor, CinemaScope). Art dir: Cedric Gibbons, Hans Peters. Mus: Miklos Rozsa. With: Stewart Granger *(Jeremy Fox),* George Sanders *(Lord Ashwood),* Joan Greenwood *(Lady Ashwood),* Viveca Lindfors *(Mrs Minton),* Jon Whiteley *(John Mohune).*

Lang's only film in CinemaScope, a ratio he describes in *Le Mépris* as 'only good for funerals and snakes'.

Lang disowns *Moonfleet,* claiming it was re-edited by MGM after his work was completed, but Luc Moullet considers his reaction too harsh: 'If he judges it with regard to his intentions, a director can completely underestimate his film if the result, although brilliant, betrays those intentions, while the spectator judges *only* the result, which is all that matters.' Moullet sees the film as owing its success, like all Lang's masterpieces, to a strong expression of both terms of its dialectic. A critical attitude which removes a romantic aura from the events and characters of the past (he compares the George Sanders character here to his counterpart in *While the City Sleeps)* is balanced by a sensibility to the kind of romanticism which characterises his earlier films.

1955 Gavin Lambert's two-part article, 'Fritz Lang's America', appeared in *Sight and Sound* (Summer/Autumn).

While the City Sleeps (RKO Teleradio). Dir: Lang. Prod: Bert Friedlob. Sc: Casey Robinson, from novel *The Bloody Spur* by Charles Einstein. Ph: Ernest Laszlo (SuperScope). Art dir: Carroll Clark. Mus: Herschel Burke Gilbert. With: Dana Andrews *(Mobley),* Rhonda Fleming *(Dorothy Kyne),* Sally Forrest *(Nancy),* Thomas Mitchell *(Griffith),* Vincent Price *(Walter Kyne Jr),* Ida Lupino *(Mildred),* George Sanders *(Mark Loving),* James Craig *(Harry Kritzer).*

When Bogdanovich suggested that the murderer was a more sympathetic character than the newspaper people, Lang replied: 'You are very romantic. They are human beings. How many people have you met in your life who are ethical? So what do you expect from these people . . .?'

But Jean Domarchi *(Cahiers du Cinéma,* October 1956) described the film as 'a contribution of the first order to the aesthetics of the abject . . . his [Lang's] icy detachment is that of the naturalist or the ethnologist. He describes a flock of crows descending on carcases, and from his statement is born a judgment without right of appeal . . . One could say that all baseness and incommensurable female foolishness arrange to meet in a grotesque and sometimes lascivious saraband. No forgiveness for humanity such as this'. And no place for naturalism: 'It hardly matters that the case considered here does not correspond to everyday reality . . . It's not a question of documentary realism . . . It's a question of an analysis which only retains certain determining details . . .'

1956 ✗ **Beyond a Reasonable Doubt** (RKO Teleradio). Prod: Bert Friedlob. Dir: Lang. Sc: Douglas Morrow. Ph: William Snyder (RKO Scope). Art dir: Carroll Clark. Mus: Herschel Burke Gilbert. With: Dana Andrews *(Tom Garrett)*, Joan Fontaine *(Susan Spencer)*, Sidney Blackmer *(Austin Spencer)*, Philip Bourneuf *(Thompson)*, Barbara Nichols *(Sally)*.

Jacques Rivette's long review of this film *(Cahiers du Cinéma,* November 1957) is translated in *Rivette: Texts and Interviews* (edited by Jonathan Rosenbaum). Rivette writes: 'What in fact do we see? . . . In the earlier films *(Fury, You Only Live Once)* innocence with all the appearances of guilt, here guilt with all the appearances of innocence. Can anyone fail to see that they're about the same thing, or at least the same question? Beyond appearances, what are guilt and innocence? Is one ever in fact innocent or guilty?'

Tzvetan Todorov in his essay 'Introduction to Verisimilitude' (in *The Poetics of Prose)* deals with the problem in structural terms: 'The revelation, that is, the truth, is incompatible with verisimilitude; as we know from a whole series of detective plots based on the tension between them. In [Lang's film] this antithesis is taken to extremes . . . Only at the end do truth and verisimilitude coincide, but this signifies the death of the character as well as the death of the narrative, which can only continue if there is a gap between truth and verisimilitude.'

Article on Lang appeared in *Films in Review* (June/July).

Lang visited Germany en route to India, where he was to make a film entitled *Taj Mahal*. The project fell through.

1958–59 **Der Tiger von Eschnapur** and **Das indische Grabmal** (C.C.C. Film-Regina, Films Criterion, Films-Rizzoli, Films-Impéria Distribution). Dir: Lang. Prod: Louise de Masure, Eberhard Meischner. Sc: Lang, Werner Jörg Lüddecke, from original scenario by Lang, Von Harbou. Ph: Richard Angst (Colorscope). Art dir: Helmut Nentwig, Willy Schatz. Mus: Michel Michelet *(Tiger)*, Gerhard Becker *(Grabmal)*. With: Debra Paget *(Seetha)*, Paul Hubschmid *(Harald Berger)*, Walter Reyer *(Chandra)*, Claus Holm *(Dr Rhode)*, Sabine Bethmann *(Irene Rhode)*, René Deltman *(Ramigani)*.

Lang's script, written with Thea von Harbou, had been filmed in 1921 by Joe May. Almost forty years later his own version divided the French critics. In a *Sight and Sound* poll in 1962, Jean Douchet placed it among the ten greatest films of all time. Fereydoun Hoveyda *(Cahiers du Cinéma*, September 1959) claimed that 'this diptych teaches us more about Lang than all his previous films, and constitutes an important work . . . the interest of the film resides essentially not in its subject, but in its *mise en scène,* and the care over stylisation. The episodes multiply and reach heights of delirium . . . Lang throws in our face from the start a determined anti-realism. In the Indian temples rebuilt in the studio, he places Europeanised dances. He turns the Maharajah of Eschnapur into an operetta prince. I find absolutely pleasing the idea of making Debra Paget dance déshabillé in a kind of Folies-Bergères . . .'
But Luc Moullet, while acknowledging the formal ambition of the films, especially the beautiful cold colours and inexorably precise découpage of the first part, finds them flawed by the absence of an internal dialectic, uninteresting script and characters, and mediocre actors.

1959 *Cahiers du Cinéma* published issue (September) devoted to Lang, containing articles, interview and filmography.
Künstlerporträt: Fritz Lang, a half-hour West German TV programme on Lang.

1960 **Die tausend Augen des Dr Mabuse** (C.C.C. Film-Criterion Films-Cei-Incom-Omnia Distribution). Dir/Prod: Lang. Sc: Lang, Heinz Oskar Wuttig. Ph: Karl Loeb. Art dir: Erich Kettelhut, Johannes Ott. Mus: Bert Grund. With: Dawn Addams *(Marion)*, Peter Van Eyck *(Travers)*, Wolfgang Preiss

170

(Jordan), Gert Fröbe *(Commissioner Kras)*, Werner Peters *(Mistelzweig)*, Lupo Prezzo *(Cornelius)*.

In a long review *(Cahiers du Cinéma*, August 1961) Jean Douchet sees Mabuse's (as he became in dubbed versions) desire for ubiquity (the bank of TV screens depicting simultaneously what is occurring in various parts of the Hotel Luxor) as the 'supreme temptation of the metteur en scène', reflecting his wish to 'bring everything back to himself . . . The enormous means at his disposal . . . are not the tools of a worker who wishes to explore and understand the world, but the instruments which will permit him to rule it . . .'

Roger Greenspun *(Film Comment*, March/April 1973) compares 'Mabuse' with Travers, since 'both men are power manipulators and both are voyeurs. However, between Travers and his one way mirror and Mabuse at the dials of his television screens there is a world of moral difference to choose. When Travers breaks through the mirror to save the love he has been visually devouring he makes a bid for freedom. He moves from behind a wall of frustrated desire to direct involvement . . . The art of seeing in the later films of Fritz Lang . . . invokes for the protagonist a decision not merely to look but rather to enter into the scene his imaginative concentration has in part called into being'.

1962   Article by John Russell Taylor, 'The Nine Lives of Dr Mabuse', published in *Sight and Sound* (Winter).
Lang retrospective at National Film Theatre, London. Article by Nicholas Garnham on Lang published in *Film* (GB) magazine.
Interview with Lang in *Movie* (no. 4).

1963   Lang appeared, as himself, in Godard's *Le Mépris*.
Luc Moullet's book *Fritz Lang* published in France.
Francis Courtade's book *Fritz Lang* published in France.
Peter Fleischmann made a 14-minute film *Begegnung mit Fritz Lang*.

1964   Lang served on the juries at the Cannes Film Festival and the Mannheim International Film Week.
Lang interviewed for one of a series of West German TV programmes, *Das war die UFA*.
Alfred Eibel's book *Fritz Lang* published in France.
Lang interviewed in *Cahiers du Cinéma* (June).
Documentation for the Bad Ems retrospective of Lang's work

published in book form in Germany.
Script of *M* published, plus essay by Lotte Eisner, in *L'Avant-Scène du Cinéma* (no. 39).

1965   Lang made 'Officier d'Art et des Lettres' in France.
First part of two-part article, 'La Nuit Viennoise. Une Confession de Fritz Lang', published in *Cahiers du Cinéma* (August). Second part published June 1966.
Chapter on Lang's German films in Eric Rhode's book *Tower of Babel*.

1967   Peter Bogdanovich's book *Fritz Lang in America* published.
Interview with Lang in *Sight and Sound* (Summer).

1968   Erwin Leiser made a 49-minute film, *Zum Beispiel Fritz Lang*, shown on West German TV.
Image et Son magazine published an issue (April) on Lang.

1969   Lang retrospective at Los Angeles County Museum.
Paul Jensen's book *The Cinema of Fritz Lang* published.
Lotte Eisner's book, *The Haunted Screen*, on German 'Expressionist' cinema, published.

1970   Article by Paul Joannides, 'Aspects of Fritz Lang', published in *Cinema* (GB) magazine (August).

1971   Three programmes on Lang by Klaus Kreimeier broadcast by West Deutscher Rundfunk TV.
Lang visited West Germany again.

1972   Colin McArthur's book *Underworld USA* published, containing section on Lang.
Article, 'Fritz Lang and the Film Noir', published in *Mise en Scène* magazine no. 1.

1973   MA thesis for University of Exeter, 'Fritz Lang: Cinema of Destiny', by Julian Petley. Unpublished.

1974   West Deutscher Rundfunk TV programme, *Die schweren Träume des Fritz Lang,* by Werner Dütsch.
Interview with Lang published in *Dialogue on Film* (April).

1976   Book, *Fritz Lang,* by Frieda Grafe, Enno Patalas, Hans Prinzler and Peter Syr, published in Germany.
Lang dies in Beverly Hills on 2 August.

Book, *Fritz Lang*, by Lotte Eisner, published.
Book, *The Films of Fritz Lang*, by Frederick W. Ott, published.
Positif magazine published issue containing material on Lang (December).

1978   Retrospective of Lang's work at National Film Theatre, London. All the director's surviving films shown, including longer versions of *Kriemhilds Rache*, *Spione* and *M*, restored by Munich Film Museum.
Article, 'The Place of Women in Fritz Lang's *The Blue Gardenia*', by E. Ann Kaplan, published in book *Women in Film Noir* (reprinted 1980).

1979   Book, *Fritz Lang*, by Robert A. Armour, published.

1980   Book, *Fritz Lang: A Research and Reference Guide*, by E. Ann Kaplan, published.